THE FARMER FROM TEKOA

the Farmer from Tekoa

ON THE BOOK OF AMOS

BY

HERMAN VELDKAMP

PAIDEIA PRESS

ST. CATHARINES, ONTARIO, CANADA

1977

First published in Dutch
as *De boer uit Tekoa*
by T. Wever of Franeker.
Translated by Theodore Plantinga.

ISBN 0-888-15-000-8
Printed in the United States of America.

Table of Contents

1.
The Farmer from Tekoa

*The words of Amos, who was among the
shepherds of Tekoa, which he saw concerning
Israel . . . (1:1).*

We know very little about Amos. All our knowledge
of him comes from the short book that bears his name, for
he does not appear elsewhere in Scripture.

All the same, it is surprising what a clear picture of his
standing we can form. Amos himself speaks of his position
twice (1:1 and 7:14).

Prophets are neither demigods nor angelic beings.
They, too, must earn a living. For them as for us, making a
living comes before philosophizing. Nowhere do the Scriptures look down on earthly things or brand them as evil.
Nowhere in the Bible is money called "filthy lucre."

The prophet Amos, the mighty man of God, opens his book in a very sober and prosaic way, then, by introducing himself to us as one of the "shepherds" of Tekoa. He begins by telling us what he does for a living.

Amos was a shepherd from Tekoa. We know that Tekoa was not too far from Bethlehem, another town famous for its shepherds. This starts us thinking of Amos as another "man of the people," someone from the working class, one of the poor, a toiler who plodded along behind his boss's sheep during hot days and chilly nights.

However poetic this picture of Amos may be, it is not correct. Reality is much more prosaic. The word in 1:1 translated as "shepherd" also occurs in II Kings 3:4, where it is applied to Mesha, the king of Moab. There it is translated as "sheep breeder." Apparently the translators of the Bible found it easy to imagine a king as a sheep breeder, but could not picture a prophet in such a role. All the same, Amos was indeed a sheep breeder.

To get still closer to the meaning of the original Hebrew word, let's call him a sheep owner. We are not told whether Amos owned a great many sheep. In any event, his farm was big enough that no king would need to be ashamed of it. It was a little kingdom by itself.

The supposition that Amos was a capable businessman and already well off is confirmed by what Amos himself said to Amaziah at Bethel (7:14-15). Amaziah accused him of trying to earn a living at Bethel by prophesying and told him to return to his own country (Judah) to earn his living there instead. Amos rejected this accusation indignantly and pointed out that he was *not* a member of the prophet's guild and did not *need* to prophesy to earn his living, for he owned enough to support himself.

How did Amos make a living? He mentions first that he was a herdsman, but immediately adds a second business in which he was involved: he was a dresser of sycamore trees. In addition to keeping animals, then, Amos was engaged in agriculture or horticulture. Besides his farm, he owned a piece of land somewhere else where he grew sycamore trees. (These trees could not be grown in Tekoa.) Thus Amos presents himself to us as an independent man with various sources of income.

We might speak of him as a well-to-do farmer — provided that the word *farmer* does not make us think of someone ignorant and uncultured. If, however, we identify "culture" with decadence, by which we mean the abandonment of ethical norms and values because of an accommodation to "culture," then Amos was certainly not a cultured man.

The cultured women of Samaria, whom this prophet condemned in an uncultured manner as "cows of Bashan," no doubt regarded him as very "crude." As a pure child of nature, a son of the wilderness, Amos could never get used to the "culture" of Samaria.

But Amos knew of a different kind of culture — that of the spirit! The Spirit of the Lord, which inspired the writers of the Bible, has always made use of the human talents and abilities of the instruments He chose. When we follow the flight of Amos's thoughts, his dramatic imagination, and his poetic prose (which we will discuss later), we are amazed that this Tekoan breeder of sheep and planter of fig trees possessed such a refined soul and sensitive heart. Thus the words of the book of Amos are the words and visions of the prophet and poet and artist and sheep breeder and sycamore planter whom we call Amos.

There is a definite danger in such a combination of talents. It is rare for anyone to be truly *talented* in two different areas. History has taught us that a shoemaker-philosopher is either a poor shoemaker or an incompetent philosopher. He must be one or the other. But Amos was an exception to this rule. He was called to be a *prophet*. Although he did not report any vision in which he was called, as other prophets have done, he did say explicitly that *the Lord* called him to be a prophet (7:15). Yet he also remained a sheep farmer. He did not give up his original vocation when he became a prophet, nor did he join the guild of those who listed their occupation as prophet. He made this very clear when he said to Amaziah, "I am no prophet, nor a prophet's son; but I am a herdsman, and a dresser of sycamore trees" (7:14).

Thus Amos made it clear that prophecy was *not* his business. When he emphasized this point he did not mean to cast aspersions on prophecy *as such,* any more than he wished to deny his prophetic calling, to which he had just drawn attention in an emphatic way. What he wanted to make Amaziah understand was that *although* he was "one of the sheep-farmers of Tekoa" (1:1 NEB) and therefore did business at the markets of Bethel and Samaria, he had nevertheless been given a Word from the Lord, a message from God. The message he proclaimed was not his own, but had been revealed to him by God.

The lion had roared. Was there anyone so foolish as not to be afraid? The Lord had spoken. Who could shrink from prophesying?

The awesome authority of Amos came from this amazing calling, this strange combination of sheep farming and prophecy. We should think of his career as prophet roughly in this way. Amos's home was in Tekoa. His business as a sheep farmer required that he make frequent visits to the markets at Jerusalem, Hebron, Bethel, and Samaria, where he bought sheep and sold wool. Consequently Amos was often away from home and spent a good deal of time with his colleagues, the "sheep-farmers of Tekoa." These farmers of Tekoa were a familiar sight in the various cities, and Amos was often among them.

In Samaria and Bethel, Amos was repeatedly exposed to the injustices, worldliness and moral degeneration of Israel. As he witnessed the social oppression of the poor and the drunkenness in the beautiful palaces, he got angry. Then, one day, in the stillness of Tekoa, the Word of the

Lord came to him. Amos heard God speaking to him just as clearly as one might hear a lion roaring in the wilderness of Judah. God had a task for Amos: he was to speak to Israel through words and visions. He was ordered to bring a message from God as he made his trips to the markets. In God's name he was to protest against the sins of Israel. He was to announce God's judgments.

At first this buyer and seller and sheep breeder must have dreaded his assignment. But what he thought or felt made no difference, for the lion had roared. The Lord had spoken! Who was Amos to refuse to prophesy?

Before long Amos was on the road again with his companions and appeared in the cities of Samaria and Bethel. This time he was driven not by the desire to do business but by the irresistible urge to proclaim God's message. In the middle of the marketplace he made himself heard. At the altars he proclaimed his message. At the festivals his words flashed like lightning.

The houses of ivory shook from the thunder of his words. Then he suddenly disappeared again. The prophet went back to his business concerns, turning his attention toward his gardens and animals. Once more it was quiet on the mountain of Samaria and people could relax — until he suddenly reappeared in Samaria's streets like a flash of lightning, uttering sharp warnings to those who were at ease.

The presence of this businessman and prophet and farmer jolted the cities in the kingdom of the ten tribes, from Bethel to Samaria. People complained that he got everyone upset.

The lion had roared!

When the people listened to Amos, whom they already knew as "one of the sheep-farmers" who came to the market regularly to do business, and when they later read his account of his visions, they were taken aback and grew suspicious. Didn't they know from experience how much one could rely on the word of those farmers at the market? Either it's too dry for them, or there's too much rain. Farmers are always complaining about prices and bad times — and Amos was no exception!

A person who becomes a prophet remains a human being. When Amos spoke as a prophet, he still talked about hard times and rain, just as he had done before, but there was something different about his words. He declared, "Thus says the Lord: 'I brought famine on all your settlements [It was not the government's doing], and I would send rain on one city and no rain on another, yet you did not come back to me' " (4:6, 7, 8 NEB). That was Yahweh's complaint and Amos's prophecy.

As for the visions, people who spend their time at the marketplace and the stock exchange are full of visions, dreams and ideals. They imagine themselves rich and seek happiness in dreams of profitable transactions. Amos had visions too. He saw Yahweh with a plumb line measuring the crookedness of Israel's walls and the injustice within those walls. That was part of his prophecy.

Amos was not a prophet because he saw things differently from his contemporaries. Nor was he a prophet because he was any more conscientious than others or could speak more piously. No, what drove him to prophesy was God's Spirit. It was the presence of the Spirit in his life that made his position completely unique.

When Amos asks who can refrain from prophesying once the Lord has spoken, we are reminded of something in the New Testament. His question points to the office of all believers. If only *all* the people of the Lord were prophets! Amos's unique way of combining sheep farming and prophecy prefigures the New Testament idea of the office of all believers.

Now, all of us, as people of the Lord, are called to be prophets, whether we are businessmen, farmers, factory workers, chauffeurs, travel agents, civil servants, janitors, or construction workers. Nevertheless, we are quick to make a distinction here. The words and visions of prophets and preachers are very different from our own, we maintain; they are more profound and eloquent and edifying. The layman thinks superficially and never gets to the heart of the matter. Thus we're eager to resign our office. How many of us have managed even *once* — to say nothing of doing so every day — to surprise those around us and make them say, "Isn't he one of the sheep farmers from Tekoa? What's come over him?"

Whenever God's Spirit takes hold of a human heart in some corner of the world, that person becomes a Christian, that is, a priest, a king, and also a prophet. Yet, when he assumes these three offices, he retains his original vocation. He remains a carpenter, a tailor, a salesman, a clothes designer, or whatever he may be. All the same, an amazing transformation takes place when he is given an additional calling or office — that of prophet. He *speaks* differently. He *sees* things differently. He testifies and prophesies and protests. These anointed prophets must see to it that the inhabitants of this poor world, those who are at ease in Zion as well as the churchgoers of Bethel, London and New York, know that there are Christians in the world, that there are prophets in Israel!

2.
The Calf
That Drowned

*. . . which he saw concerning Israel in the days
of Uzziah king of Judah and in the days of
Jeroboam the son of Joash, king of Israel, two
years before the earthquake (1:1).*

Our first chapter was entitled "The Farmer from
Tekoa." We now continue this line of thought under the
heading "The Calf That Drowned."

We need not point the finger at some stupid farmer
who asked for trouble by forgetting to put a cover on his
well. No, the stupidity was the work of the cultured ladies
and gentlemen who lived in the cities of the kingdom of the
ten tribes, the same people who liked to make fun of that

foolish farmer Amos. They said, "He should tend to his sheep and not bother us with his crazy ideas."

After all, who in his right mind talks about falling into wells that don't exist? Who worries about bad weather when there isn't a cloud in the sky? Yet, that's what Amos is doing! Just listen to him once. First he talks about bad weather, and then about a clear sky.

Amos's prediction of bad weather was not without foundation. There was rumbling and crackling to be heard on all sides; there were ominous sounds in the sky above and on the earth.. The very beginning of his book already breathed calamity, for he spoke of what he saw "*two years before the earthquake.*" This remained the framework of all of his prophecy: earthquake, misfortune, destruction.

His younger contemporary Hosea sang to Israel the song of God's love, but Amos's mouth was filled with the cry of vengeance. Hosea's flute invited Israel to dance, but Amos's lament called for breast-beating.

Amos witnessed the dark clouds of God's judgment forming. There was hardly a ray of light to be seen. (Only the last five verses of the last chapter contain promises.)

Amos called for repentance and prophesied judgment. Thus his name was appropriate, for *Amos* means *one who bears a burden.* That burden was to prophesy to his *own people* about their destruction. (Although Amos himself came from Judah and preached judgment mainly to the ten tribes, Israel was still a brother nation.) Who could bear such a burden?

Amos bore his burden manfully. Faithfully he made his message heard. In the cities of Israel he cried out:

See then how I am going to crush you into the ground
as the threshing sledge crushes when clogged by straw;
flight will not save even the swift,
the strong man will find his strength useless,
the mighty man will be powerless to save himself (2:13-14 JB).

Amos also warned:

> An enemy shall surround the land;
> your stronghold shall be thrown down
> and your palaces sacked (3:11 NEB).

Those who survived this holocaust would have to go into exile "beyond Damascus," Amos declared, on behalf of the Lord, "whose name is the God of hosts" (5:27). When that time comes, the earth will quake and shake, making the catastrophe complete. The feeling of panic will be so great that the rich, who seem so serene and confident today, will run away with a scant bundle of goods in their arms, like refugees fleeing the advance of a conquering army. "Thus says the Lord: 'As the shepherd rescues from the mouth of the lion two legs, or a piece of an ear, so shall the people of Israel who dwell in Samaria be rescued, with the corner of a couch and part of a bed' " (3:12).

Did Amos already have Assyria in mind when he spoke of enemies approaching? I leave this question for exegetical scholars to answer, together with the question whether Amos himself had predicted the earthquake of which he spoke. Neither question is answered in the text.

The reason Amos's words were so frightening was that the calamity was not spelled out clearly. "The catastrophe is on the way," he warned. What a dreadful thing to say! "Does the trumpet sound in the city without the populace becoming alarmed?" (3:6 JB).

No, Israel is not afraid. Israel is roaring with laughter. Let Amos forecast as much bad weather as he likes. Weather forecasts are always wrong, anyway. Isn't the sky perfectly clear and blue? Is there a single sign pointing to an impending calamity? No, not one.

You yourself must admit it, Amos. It doesn't look as though you're right.

What about that clear sky? Never had the sun shone so brightly on the promised land as in the time of Jeroboam II and Uzziah. Never did people sit so contentedly in the shade of fig trees and vines as when Uzziah reigned over Judah and Jeroboam, the son of Joash, reigned over Israel (i.e., about 750 B.C.).* It was as though the golden age of Solomon had returned. The deplorable civil disputes of an earlier era had ended, and peace was restored within the land. Syria, Israel's traditional enemy, had been completely conquered by Jeroboam. Although Jehu, an earlier king, had been forced to make payments to the mighty Assyrians, the power of the Assyrians had declined during Jeroboam's time. There was no longer any danger to fear from the north (Assyria) or from the south.

Jeroboam II was the most successful king Israel had ever had. Even Uzziah, who ruled in Judah, shared somewhat in his glory. It was a time of glittering prosperity, a great time to be alive. Business flourished, and people made a lot of money. Many were wealthy enough to maintain both a winter home and a summer home and could even afford the luxury of costly ivory to adorn the walls of their homes and decorate the couches on which they lay to eat their meals (3:15 and 6:4).

The people who had once lived a nomadic life had become a cultured nation. The slaves of yesteryear had become property owners. Jewels adorned the fingers and hands that had once been callous from making bricks. The nation that had earlier been in bondage could congratulate itself at its religious feasts, for it had come a long way and its star was rising.

Then along came Amos with his wild talk. Prophets are always pessimists! What Amos was saying was madness; it was the height of naiveté. Was it conceivable that a nation which had crushed the Syrians and expanded its borders as

---

*Although Amos prophesied mainly against the northern kingdom of the ten tribes, where Jeroboam II was king, he also mentioned Uzziah, the king of Judah, at the beginning of his book of prophecy, probably to avoid creating the impression that he prophesied against Israel for political reasons. It would be easy to reach such a conclusion about someone from Judah.

never before would go into exile? Was there any reason at all for making such somber predictions?

Surely everyone had to admit that what Amos wrote at the beginning of his book didn't make sense. Talk of an earthquake was simply out of place during the glorious days of the second Jeroboam. A clear sky means good weather. Because those who lived on the mountain of Samaria were so sure of this, they relaxed. They believed that the evil day was far away (6:1, 3).

In those days, when the sun kissed the flowers and made the ivory palaces gleam, the prophet of doom who walked the streets of Samaria and Bethel preaching that judgment was at hand soon became the chief topic of conversation. Some laughed or shrugged their shoulders as they saw him pass, thinking him a strange character. When people visited each other, they talked about Amos, making fun of him as they drank their wine. Finally one of the ladies suggested that they drink a toast to the health of this sheep dealer from Tekoa (4:1). But the men, who were not altogether at ease, answered, "Why doesn't he look after his sheep and stop bothering us with his crazy ideas?"

Yet what Amos had to say was not so crazy. It's true that everything appeared to be in perfect order — also in religious respects! Never were so many voluntary sacrifices made (4:5). Large groups of pilgrims traveled through the land to visit the holy places. But that's exactly what was wrong. A time of success and external splendor has never been a time in which the faith of the church grew and blossomed. When the church buildings are made of gold, the Christians in the pew are made of wood at best. Actually, they look more like pieces of rotten wood.

Perhaps we could compare Israel to a piece of mahogany furniture on which termites have been chewing. Therefore we should not act surprised when we read that there was an earthquake: what should surprise us instead is that two years went by before it took place. God was certainly merciful.

The prophet Amos paints a sad picture of the *inner* decay that had taken place, despite the beautiful appearance. There was a deep abyss between Israel's doctrine and its life. Those Israelites seemed such pious believers — but the sacrifices they brought to the Lord were *stolen:* they were wrung from the defenseless poor.

Amos directed his greatest wrath against *social* injustice. Although he was not a socialist, equating wealth itself with sin, he warned that Joseph's house would collapse because Israel's wealth was squeezed out of the poor, because the needy were sold into slavery for the price of a pair of shoes.

Prominent city-dwellers trampled upon the poor and demanded exorbitant interest on the money owed them (5:11), singing the psalms of David all the while! (6:5). Merchants used false weights and measures. On the sabbath day they waited eagerly for the sun to set so they would be allowed to return to their work (8:4-6), still singing David's psalms! All down the line Amos saw corruption.

The judges accepted bribes (5:12). Scandalous immorality was the order of the day (2:6). Licentiousness and heavy drinking were what made life worth living (4:1), while everyone sang the psalms of David!

These pious scoundrels of Zion were so much at ease that they even looked forward to the "day of the Lord" (5:18), believing that God's lightning would only strike the world of the heathens, leaving the palaces of the "chosen people" untouched. Such offenses cried out to heaven and made the catastrophe inevitable. Therefore the beginning of Amos's book, which mentions both Jeroboam's glory and the approaching misery, is not so strange after all.

The judgment announced by Amos was realized fully when Israel was conquered and sent into exile. Even before then, the "earthquake" had given the Israelites an indication of what they were in for. We know nothing about this "earthquake" but what Amos tells us. There is, however, an ancient Assyrian text which speaks of an *eclipse of the sun,* which Amos also mentions (8:9). This testifies in a remarkable way to the truth of the Biblical record. Astronomers in our time have been able to figure out the exact date: June 15, 763 B.C., which was during the time of Jeroboam.

Whenever the earthquake occurred, it was a major catastrophe. This is already obvious from the fact that Amos speaks of it simply as "the" earthquake. Apparently everyone knew exactly what event he was talking about. So clearly did the people of Israel remember this earthquake that Zechariah could still threaten them after the exile by saying, "You shall flee as you fled from the earthquake in the days of Uzziah king of Judah" (Zech. 14:5).

One day the horrible event suddenly took place. The land became turbulent like the sea, as the summer and winter homes collapsed. There was cracking and groaning and tearing to be heard on all sides. People fled with their possessions in their arms. Where were they going? They were running into the arms of death.

The ladies and gentlemen of Samaria then stopped making fun of Amos and drinking mock toasts to him. His words "Thus says the Lord" kept ringing in their ears. But by then the calf had already drowned — together with many of the people — and it was too late to cover the well.

The most terrible of the judgments announced by Amos was the following:

"Behold, the days are coming," says the Lord God,
"when I will send a famine on the land;
not a famine of bread, nor a thirst for water,
but of hearing the words of the Lord.
They shall wander from sea to sea,
and from north to east;
they shall run to and fro, to seek the word of the Lord,
but they shall not find it" (8:11-12).

This was indeed a dreadful judgment! It was worse than earthquakes, plagues, wars, or economic crises.

God chooses His own time for His Words. That time
is not when man in his desperation seeks God's Words
but when God in His mercy sends them. That time — in
the case we are considering — was two years before the
earthquake. In those two years God still gave His people a
chance, but once those years were over it was too late.
People searched, but they did not find what they were
looking for.

"Hear this word, you cows of Bashan!" Remember
the calf that drowned.

No doubt people became "interested" in the words and
visions of Amos *after* the earthquake. Suddenly the much
maligned farmer from Tekoa was in demand. Therefore
the prophet who preached also put his message down in
writing. But the words he wrote had little effect on his contemporaries. This hardening of their hearts was also a
judgment!

When the Holy Spirit inspired Amos to become a writer
of God's Words, His purpose must have been for *us* to
hear them, for we are still living *before* the earthquake —
the earthquake that will inaugurate the great day of the
Lord, when we will hear of wars, rumors of wars, and
earthquakes in various places.

And although many believe the evil day is still far
away, we already hear rumbling underground. A cloudless
sky is no guarantee that lightning will not strike. "I shall
come like a thief in the night."

We still live *before* "the" earthquake. Who can say
when it will happen? Do we have two years left, or ten years,
or twenty years? In any event, it will come as soon as the
time the Lord has given us for repentance has passed.

Do you and I still need to repent? Yes we do — *all* of
us. We need every day that God allows us.

Isn't there a lot of outward activity in our lives that covers
inward rottenness? Don't the lives of many of us give the
lie to our confession? Isn't there at least one sin in your life
of which you must still repent?

Don't forget that God's Words choose their own time. That time is now — two years before the earthquake. Don't forget that the hardening of hearts is also a judgment. Remember the calf that drowned!

3.
Gilead's Trail of Blood

For three transgressions of Damascus . . . (1:3).

There are people who are in the habit of paying careful attention to the first half of the sermon and falling asleep during the second half. If there were such people in Samaria's streets as Amos preached there one day, they must have regarded the sermon as splendid.

Amos, they thought, can really lay it on the line. There's no doubt about it: he's a powerful speaker, a people's preacher.

From the crowd that had gathered came approving murmurs and cries of "Amen!" And it was indeed a powerful sermon. Wasn't Amos pronouncing God's judgment on the "world"? Wasn't he announcing what God would do to the heathens, His ancient enemies?

Just listen to what this wilderness preacher is saying. He declares that the Lord has kept His silence about the atrocities of the heathens long enough. Now He will roar from Zion and make His voice heard (1:2). God's storm clouds are gathering. His lightning illuminates the world — and strikes.

The first words are about the palaces of Damascus, the capital city of the heathen Syrians, those traditional enemies of Israel:

> For three transgressions of Damascus,
> and for four, I will not revoke the punishment.

The listeners understood what Amos meant. One of these atrocities was enough in itself to earn the death penalty, but Damascus was guilty of much more. Because it had committed three or four of these offenses, each one calling for the death penalty, the judgment was irrevocable and could not be appealed. There was no longer any escape possible for Damascus.

And when Amos was finished with the Syrians in Damascus, he turned to the Philistines, the inhabitants of Gaza:

> For three transgressions of Gaza,
> and for four, I will not revoke the punishment (1:6).

Then followed the endless series: The Phoenicians, the Edomites, the Ammonites, the Moabites. Lightning flashed through the air and consumed the palaces of Tyre, Bozrah, Rabbah, and Kerioth (1:9 — 2:3). The homes and cities of the heathens went up in smoke.

That's what we like to hear, Amos! May all those confident heathens perish!

The loud voice of Amos preaching in the street penetrated clearly into the living room of one of those "houses of ivory," where some residents of Samaria were reclining on couches and having a drink. They nodded at each other. "This time Amos has really told it to those enemies of God," said one. "What a man!" Another, sipping at his drink, muttered something about "the evil world." Then he stretched out on his couch and fell asleep.

If he had *not* done so and had *not* taken such pleasure in what Amos said about the evil world, which is so far away anyway, but had listened carefully to the rest of the sermon, he might well have become uneasy. During the first half of the sermon, when Amos was talking about the "world," a sensitive listener could already have figured out that something was amiss. He could have seen it coming. The storm could not stand still over the lands of the heathens. It would get closer and closer, until the lightning struck Jerusalem and Samaria.

There is an obvious climax in this sermon of Amos, which is recorded in the first two chapters of his book. As long as he talked about Tyre, he was a comfortable distance away. But then, as he condemned nation after nation, he turned to the nations related to Israel by *blood,* i.e., Edom, Ammon, and Moab. These nations were the descendants of Esau and Lot. Amos kept getting closer and closer. Finally he arrived at his goal. The prophecy of judgment against the surrounding nations was really a deliberate *introduction* to his condemnation of Judah and Israel. The thunder rumbling in the distance was a preparation:

For three transgressions of *Judah* . . . .

For three transgressions of *Israel* . . . .

People of God, he means you! God's lightning will strike you hardest of all.

When the preacher reached the climax of his sermon, some people tapped their heads and said, "He's got something missing up there." Their approval turned to hostility. It turned out to be a poor sermon after all. Some of them laughed. A few became uneasy.

God's prophets are not one-sided. The sinful Israelites were not to think that God's judgment would strike *only* the heathens, sparing them because they were "children of Abraham."

On the other hand, the heathens did have every reason to tremble. The world was not to think that God would remain silent *forever*. Even though this entire prophecy of judgment ultimately led to God's "covenant people," the heathens would not be overlooked. God's wrath would also strike them.

In punishing the heathens, God once more showed His *mercy* toward His deeply sinful people. The striking thing about Amos's judgment sermon against the *heathens* is that the offenses for which the Judge of heaven and earth condemned them to death were offenses against *His people!*

> Because they have threshed Gilead . . . (1:3).
> Because they carried into exile a whole people . . . (1:6, 9).
> Because Edom pursued his brother with the sword . . . (1:11).

These misdeeds cried out for the death penalty. With a mother's tenderness, the Lord took the side of "His people"!

On the other hand, the Lord does not spare His people or exempt them from His wrath. He refuses to put up with their sinful ways. But He is also enraged when the heathens take up arms against His people and mutilate them. This makes Him roar like a lioness robbed of her young. Then He takes the side of His people, as a mother takes the side of the children who caused her so much sorrow and deserted her.

God is stern as a father when He is angry at His children, but tender as a mother as He protects the children who have abandoned Him. Remember that, you heathens! Be careful! Don't lay a finger on the apple of His eye! It may be that Gilead is a city of evildoers, full of bloody footprints (Hosea 6:8), but that does not give you the right to trample it underfoot, Damascus. Gilead is the Lord's!

Vengeance is mine, the Lord declares. I will repay. If you don't keep your hands off My people, Damascus, then hear this:

For three transgressions of Damascus,
and for four, I will not revoke the punishment;
because they have threshed Gilead
with threshing sledges of iron.
So I will send a fire upon the house of Hazael,
and it shall devour the strongholds of Ben-hadad (1:3-4).

The offense that Syria had dared to commit against God's people was particularly barbarous. These Syrians, or Aramaeans, are here referred to as "Damascus," their capital city, just as we sometimes speak of "Paris" when we mean France. Amos mentioned two rulers of this kingdom by name. Hazael was the founder of the Syrian dynasty. It was the prophet Elisha who had designated him to be king over Syria. Hazael was a particularly barbaric man. We read that Elisha wept when he foresaw in the spirit what evil this Hazael was to do to the children of Israel. When Hazael asked him why he was weeping, he replied, "Because I know the evil that you will do to the people of Israel; you will set on fire their fortresses, and you will slay their young men with the sword, and dash in pieces their little ones, and rip up their women with child" (II Kings 8:12). This barbarian revealed his nature when he invaded the land east of the Jordan while Jehu was king (II Kings 10:32-3), for he murdered the inhabitants of Gilead in a horrible way. The people of Gilead were forced to lie on the ground. Then heavy iron threshing machines equipped with sharp iron knives went to work on this living field, turning it into a bloody mass of flesh.

This is what Israel's poet lamented when he wrote:
The plowers plowed upon my back;
they made long their furrows (Ps. 129:3).

Horrible! This story is all the more sickening when we remember that the Syrians did this to a people that had always dealt with them in a surprisingly gentle way. Had Ben-hadad's men not been treated well when they came to Israel's king with ropes on their heads after hearing that the kings of Israel were gracious? (I Kings 20:31-4). And

when the entire army of the Syrians once fell into the hands
of Israel's king, what happened? Were all the Syrian soldiers
slaughtered? No, we read that the king "prepared for them
a great feast; and when they had eaten and drunk, he sent
them away, and they went to their master" (II Kings 6:23).
Hazael showed his gratitude for these favors by mutilating
the inhabitants of Gilead with his heavy iron threshing
machines. Ingratitude is the *world's* idea of repayment.

All of this had taken place some time ago, during the
reign of Jehu. In Damascus most of it had already been
forgotten. But the Lord does not forget. He records these
things. He brings up forgotten misdeeds from the gray past
to remind frightened sinners of them. He throws their
transgressions back at them with the words "Thus says the
Lord."

Mankind is divided into two opposing groups — and I
don't mean the proletariat and the capitalists. The two
groups are the believers and the unbelievers. Therefore the
Body of Christ should not expect to be treated differently
than Gilead was treated by Hazael and Ben-hadad.

Yet this barbarous ingratitude sometimes *disguises* itself. There are times when Ben-hadad and Ahab co-operate,
when Samaria makes an agreement with Damascus, when
the king of Israel says, "Ben-hadad is my brother" (I Kings
20:32). Then there is "covenant," and we ask ourselves,
somewhat perplexed, if it is really true — as Jesus said —
that the world will hate us as it hated Him.

Are you completely blind? Can't you see the bloody
trail of the tormented children of God running from the
ground in Palestine's Gilead through Armenia to Nero's
arena, continuing through the torture chambers of the
Spanish inquisition to the embattled Christians of Russia
and the martyred Christians in the concentration camps of
Siberia? Don't you see the trail of blood? Don't you see
the threshing machines of Gilead in their modernized forms,
which are just as barbarous?

The church would be foolish to expect anything else from the coming Hazael-Antichrist, for he will equip himself with the most modern instruments of torture and destruction. The corpses of God's people "will lie in the main street of the Great City known by the symbolic names Sodom and Egypt, in which their Lord was crucified" (Rev. 11:8 JB).

All of this goes on while our Lord, the merciful King of Israel, comes to the world in an incredibly gentle way with His hands outstretched in blessing, preparing a meal for the world, while the church does nothing but raise its hands to heaven in prayer in a priestly effort to win a blessing for the world.

The world's repayment for this is ingratitude. Therefore the judgment on Damascus is irrevocable:

> "So I will send a fire upon the house of Hazael,
> and it shall devour the strongholds of Ben-hadad.
> I will break the bar of Damascus,
> and cut off the inhabitants from the Valley of Aven,
> and him that holds the scepter from Beth-eden;
> and the people of Syria shall go into exile to Kir,"
> says the Lord (1:4-5).

This judgment doesn't leave much to the imagination. Hazael's house or dynasty — just as we speak of the *House* of Orange when we mean the royal family of the Netherlands — will be completely destroyed by the consuming fire of the lightning sent by God in judgment. Just as a fortress in ancient times had to be surrendered when the bolt barring the gate to the city was dislodged, so the bolt barring the way into Damascus will be broken by God. And when the capital city falls, the whole kingdom falls.

The judgment applies to both ruler and nation; it applies not just to the one holding the scepter but to all the people. The entire population will be wiped out. In the face of God's judgment, the distinction between a ruler and his subjects disappears. Even rulers, with all their wealth and splendor, must lay down their diadem and scepter when they face the Judge of the entire earth.

An interesting feature of this passage of judgment is a pair of names: *Valley of Aven* means *valley of sin*. *Beth-eden* means *house of pleasure*.

At this point the seer Amos broadens his vision. He sees the great day of Yahweh. He sees a great, all-encompassing fire as the Lord's lightning strikes the palaces and cottages, as the people groan in pain and implore the hills to cover them. That will be a great and terrible day.

"And the people of Syria shall go into exile to Kir," says the Lord. If some scholars are right in assuming that Kir, the place of exile of the Syrians, is none other than Ur of the Chaldees in southern Babylon, then we see God's judgment in an interesting light. It was from Ur of the Chaldees that God led the children of Israel to Palestine. He also led the Syrians out of Ur of the Chaldees once (9:7). Both the Syrians and the Israelites were promoted by God. Both the tormentors and the tormented, the conquerors and the conquered, the world and the Church, were led out of Ur. But what happened after that? The conquerors suffered a humiliating defeat. They were driven back to Kir, which they had left so long ago. What about the tormented children of Israel? God did not drive them back to Ur. Instead He promoted them once more and prepared a triumphant journey for them. They looked to the heavens and waited for the city with foundations, whose Builder and Maker is God. The path the world follows ends with a humiliation — back to Kir. The path the Church follows ends with a royal promotion: the Church enters the New Jerusalem and inherits a kingdom. The route the world follows is: from Kir to Damascus and back to Kir. The route the Church follows is: from Kir to Damascus to Jerusalem! Its route leads to a new heaven and a new earth!

Is that where you'll wind up, too? The Syrians, you must remember, were humiliated and driven back to Kir because they had become *enemies of God's people*. That was *their* sin. Is it also *your* sin? Let's focus our full attention on this cardinal question: What is my relationship to God's people? Naturally you don't run over your brother with a heavy threshing machine. But thete are so many refined forms of brutality, so many subtle ways of tormenting your brother. We all know it!

But even more important is this question: What is your relationship to the Lord Himself? Be very, very careful! Ask yourself: Have I run over the merciful King and gentle Savior with the heavy iron threshing machine of my sins? Have I made Him writhe with pain? Have I cut Him to pieces and treated Him like a worm? Be very careful as you think out your answer.

Am I any better than Hazael and Ben-hadad and that whole gang of bloodthirsty Syrians with their threshing machines in Gilead? No, not a bit.

If you can make this confession, if these questions make you feel ashamed, then a miracle will occur. The blood that flows from the Tormented One because of the threshing machines of Gilead will become a *balm* in Gilead. He will bind our wounds and heal our afflictions.

4.
Breach
of Contract

For three transgressions of Gaza . . . (1:6).
For three transgressions of Tyre . . . (1:9).

Amos could well have written a book like *Uncle Tom's Cabin,* for the prophet from Tekoa witnessed many scenes no less horrible than those described in this famous classic of slavery.

It often happened that bands of robbers and kidnapers from the Philistine city of Gaza made raids in the neighboring land of Judah. These bandits attacked defenseless villages and dragged women and children from their homes. The men were put in heavy chains and taken away. Weaklings and old men were driven along by the whips of those fierce invaders. In this way the whole pitiful procession traveled to Gaza, where there was a big slave market.

In Gaza the slave hunters and slave traders got together to do business. The slave dealers were Edomites, who were children of Esau and grandchildren of Isaac! In their quest for profits in the buying and selling of human beings, these Edomites visited not only the slave market in Gaza but also the one in Tyre (1:6, 9).

Israelites forced into slavery were inspected by slave dealers and sold. Wives were separated from their husbands. Their backs bent under the cutting lash of the whip, Israelites were transported far across the sea to the Greeks (Joel 3:6) and many heathen territories. Those who were separated from their loved ones would never be reunited.

Amos saw and heard all of this: mothers wringing their hands in despair, children whining in fear, angry men shaking their fists, old men feeling helpless, slave dealers sneering at their living merchandise, the copper chains of the captives rattling, the silver and gold gleaming in the purses of the slave traders. Business was booming!

Listen now to the sheep dealer from Tekoa as he raises his voice against the dealers in "human livestock" at Gaza and Tyre. Amos's anger resulted not so much from sympathy for the Israelite slaves as from his indignation at the *infringement* on the *rights of his God.* Had not God Himself already decreed the death penalty for stealing and selling a single human being? (Ex. 21:16). What would He say about this gruesome trade in entire populations?

The last straw was that these heathens did this to God's own children, the people He Himself had freed from slavery with His outstretched arm. The arm of the Lord had rescued the children of Israel from bondage. Now the hands of men put them in chains again and sold them into slavery. Therefore Amos thundered:

> For three transgressions of Gaza,
> and for four, I will not revoke the punishment;
> because they carried into exile a whole people
> to deliver them up to Edom.

He went on:

> For three transgressions of Tyre,
> and for four, I will not revoke the punishment;
> because they delivered up a whole people to Edom,
> and did not remember the covenant of brotherhood.

God moves in a mysterious way. The Philistines had originally become slave dealers because of the sins of the Israelites and their rulers, especially King Jehoram. We read: "And *the Lord stirred up* against Jehoram the anger of the Philistines, . . . and they came up against Judah, and invaded it, and carried away all the possessions they found that belonged to the king's house, and also his sons and his wives" (II Chron. 21:16, 17). How could the Lord now send fire upon those who were driven by His Spirit to carry out His will? It's almost beyond our comprehension.

Yet there is divine logic at work here: the Philistines went further than God intended. They exceeded the limits of their assignment as they carried out His will. The Lord's intention was to purify His people through this punishment, while the Philistines' intention was to *annihilate* their archenemies.

The Lord therefore had to intervene. Again He restored His tormented children, directing His wrath against the wrathful. Gaza and Tyre had to be reminded that they could not do as they pleased. Through the mouth of Joel, the Lord had earlier declared: "What are you to *me,* O Tyre and Sidon? For you have taken *my* silver and *my* gold, and have carried *my* rich treasures into your temples. You have sold the people of Judah and Jerusalem to the Greeks, removing them far from their own border" (Joel 3:4, 5-6). He now informed them:

> Therefore will I send fire upon the walls of Gaza,
> fire that shall consume its palaces.
> I will wipe out those who live in Ashdod
> and the sceptered ruler of Ashkelon;
> I will turn my hand against Ekron,
> and the remnant of the Philistines shall perish.
> It is the word of the Lord God (1:7-8 NEB).

So much for the glorious principalities of the Philistines: Gaza, Ashdod, Ashkelon, Ekron, as well as the city of Gath, which was not mentioned. The remnant of the Philistines would perish!

The Lord also said:

> I will send a fire upon the wall of Tyre,
> and it shall devour her strongholds (1:10).

The Edomites, who were slave dealers by profession, buying and selling human beings wholesale, were not condemned in this passage. But the Edomites would soon get their turn.

For the present, the judgment concerned only the Philistines and the Phoenicians, who sold the martyred children of God at their slave markets in Gaza and Tyre. The sins of these two peoples were identical. The same charges were made against Gaza (1:6-8) as against Tyre (1:9-10).

The Phoenicians found themselves in a slightly better position in that slave-trading was the only charge against them. (The Philistines were already guilty of other transgressions before they took up the slave trade.) But the Phoenicians made matters worse for themselves because *their* slave-trading represented a *breach of contract*. It violated an agreement, a bond between brothers. The accusation against them read:

> Because they delivered up a whole people to Edom,
> and did not remember the *covenant of brotherhood*.

That certainly strikes us as strange! Can there be a "covenant of brotherhood" between Israel and the heathens, between the church and the world? Hasn't the isolation of God's people been their source of strength throughout the ages? Can such a "covenant of brotherhood" ever be justified? If not, how can the Lord appeal to such a covenant now and reproach Tyre for breaking the covenant? Wouldn't this puzzle even the angels in heaven?

Obviously the fraternal relationship between Israel and this heathen nation was not a covenant in the deepest sense. Israel already had a covenant partner. Because Israel had entered into a firm covenant with the Lord God, it did not need any other covenant partners. When emissaries came to Jerusalem from the Philistines or any other nation to establish a covenant relationship, they were sent away with the message: "The Lord has founded Zion, and in her the afflicted of his people find refuge" (Is. 14:32). Whenever the Israelites allied themselves with surrounding nations to defend themselves against a common enemy, the prophets declared that such a foreign policy represented weakness rather than strength, that it was a sign of unbelief and distrust, and that the Israelites would collapse if they leaned on such a cane. Thus a covenant in the deepest sense cannot be what Amos meant, for the Lord would not have stood for it.

The "covenant" spoken of here is a mere trade agreement that Solomon had once made with Hiram of Tyre. In no way did it involve unbelief or any misdeed. The agreement between Solomon and Hiram included a number of provisions about trade, like the provisions any Christian businessman today might include in a contract with "worldly" people. Apparently one of the provisions dealt with the "slave trade." Solomon then bowed to the prevailing customs by calling Hiram his "brother" (I Kings 9:13), a courteous gesture that must not be seen as an expression of true brotherhood.

It appears that this trade agreement was still in effect in the time of Amos, never having been terminated. But one day Tyre began to deal in Israelite slaves, violating the provisions of the agreement and reducing it to a mere scrap of paper.

The Lord roared like a lion because of this breach of contract. Because a promise had been broken, He declared that He would send upon Tyre's wall a fire that would devour her strongholds!

Here we see the lightning flashes of God's Word illuminating what we like to call "all the areas of life." The Word of the Lord doesn't only feed the "soul"; it isn't concerned exclusively with spiritual edification. In this passage we hear God's prophet making demands about international relations and commerce (by insisting that treaties and trade agreements be kept) and about social issues as well (by declaring contracts to be binding and condemning slavery).

This is nothing new to us. Time and again we say to each other that God's Word contains "principles" for every area of life, and that we must propagate those principles. We love those "principles" and defend them loyally. But we are not so enthusiastic when it comes to applying them. Then we say, "Of course the Bible is beautiful. I read it three times each day. I hear it read Sundays in church, and I love listening to sermons — as long as I'm in church!" But once we're out of church and back on the job, drawing up contracts, making agreements about wages, concluding business deals, and so forth, we are quick to point out that it's important to look at things in a sober, objective, businesslike manner.

But the Bible wants to tell you and me some painful, sober, down-to-earth things; it wants to speak with us in private about ordinary matters like trade agreements and contracts. Perhaps we could put it this way. Our God reads contracts very carefully. He burns the palaces of those who believe they can do as they see fit. He reduces their houses of trade to rubble.

Unfortunately, the great "heathen" sin of Tyre that made God so angry is imitated in "Christian" circles. We, too, are guilty of "breach of contract"! It makes no difference whether the agreement is verbal or written. For the Christian, *every* word should be regarded as an oath, something as weighty in content as a covenant. It makes no difference whether the agreement was reached with "a brother" or with someone from "the world." The Christian should treat both as brothers when he enters into agreements with them.

Take a look at all those bits of paper from torn-up contracts swirling around in the air. Here we have a debtor who refuses to repay his loan. There we have an employer who suddenly lays off a faithful worker. All of this is done so lightly and casually by people who try to excuse themselves by talking about the need to economize and the economic crisis that can't be far away, believing that this will silence their conscience. All those people at ease on the mountain of Samaria don't even hear God thundering when He says, "I shall send a fire upon the wall of Tyre, for you have forgotten about the agreements you made."

Are you surprised when you see the remains of the walls destroyed by fire? Didn't you know that the Lord God checks up on your books and agreements, your papers and records? Didn't you know that God was the silent witness to the trade agreement between Solomon and Hiram? Didn't you know that God is objective in such matters?

The Lord does not thunder only against breach of contract and broken promises and dishonesty. He is also opposed to *slavery*. That was Gaza's special transgression. Only Gaza? "Come now," you say, "slavery was abolished long ago, and Uncle Tom's Cabin has been torn down." Do you really believe that? Do you suppose that the Lord of Hosts doesn't hear the cries of the slaves in chains? I tell you He does hear them. Think of the slavery which Nazi Germany imposed on the young men of occupied Europe during World War II. Think of the wholesale slavery that now goes on behind the Iron Curtain. But let's look closer to home!

There are white domestic slaves in many "Christian" marriages. The Roman emperor Nero first treated his wife Poppaea like a slave, then murdered her, and after her death made a goddess of her. Don't a lot of Christians play the same game? Haven't you heard about the wife who never succeeded in touching a responsive chord in her husband's heart? She was a slave to his passions and the drudge who kept house for him. She did the work and put up with the abuse. After her death, the deeply bereaved husband declared that no man could hope for a better wife — and six months later he remarried. By then he had already turned his first Poppaea into a goddess.

We have seen that God judged the heathen Philistines and Phoenicians. But mercy tempers judgment. Our God acts in amazing ways. Soon He will again move the spirit of the Philistines through His Spirit; He will move the Philistines not to beat the Israelite slaves but to give them the kiss of love. And the Phoenicians, who violated the covenant of brotherhood, will be included in a much better covenant with the children of Zion.

When God's Spirit is poured out over all flesh, what the psalmist saw from afar will be fulfilled:

> Philistine, Tyrian and Nubian shall be there;
> and Zion shall be called a mother
> in whom men of every race are born (Ps. 87:4-5 NEB).

Children of the kingdom, be careful you do not lose your place to Gaza and Tyre for failing to honor contracts and promises.

5.
Two Kinds
of Wisdom

For three transgressions of Edom . . . (1:11).

Wise men once came to Palestine from the East, probably from the area of the Tigris and Euphrates Rivers. They
were looking for the One who had been born King of the
Jews and wanted to worship Him. That was true wisdom.

The Bible also tells us about some other wise men.
These wise men did not live far away; in fact, they were
within easy reach of Bethlehem. They were the Edomites,
who were a wise people. The Temanites, who lived in the
western part of Edom, were especially renowned for their
wisdom. At one point, we hear the Lord asking, "Is wisdom
no longer to be found in Teman? Have her sages no skill in
counsel?" (Jer. 49:7 NEB). In Obadiah we read that the
Lord will "destroy all the sages of Edom and leave no wisdom on the mount of Esau" (vs. 8 NEB). The wise man

Eliphaz, whom we meet in the book of Job, was also a Temanite.

But there was something different about this wisdom of the Edomites. While the wise men from the East wanted to worship the newly-born Savior, the wise men from Edom tried to kill Him. Whereas Eastern wisdom, under the influence of the prophecy of Micah (i.e., God's revelation), culminated in a *prayer* at Bethlehem, the wisdom of the Edomites, which is from below, did not result in anything higher than the *slaughter* at Bethlehem — even though human wisdom cries aloud for "Peace on earth."

The birth of Christ laid bare the complete opposition between Eastern wisdom and Edomite wisdom, between the wisdom from above, which worships the foolishness of the manger and the cross, and the wisdom from below, which regards the foolishness of the cross as an offense. These two kinds of wisdom, that of the East and that of the Edomites, met in Jerusalem. Wasn't Herod, who was responsible for the slaughter at Bethlehem, an Idumean, that is, an Edomite and a descendant of Esau?

The true wise men decided to pray, but the Edomites in their wisdom devised a plan to murder Jesus. Now, this wasn't the first time a plan to murder the holy Seed had taken shape in Edom's fertile brain. Herod's Edomite forefathers were just like him. Long before they already tried to murder the ancestors of the holy child Jesus and made blood flow in the streets of Bethlehem. Look at the picture of the Edomites drawn by Amos:

> For three transgressions of Edom,
> and for four, I will not revoke the punishment;
> because he pursued his brother with the sword,
> and cast off all pity,
> and his anger tore perpetually,
> and he kept his wrath for ever.

Herod's slaughter at Bethlehem was the ultimate outcome of his Edomite forefathers' eternal hatred of the people of the Lord.

"For three transgressions of Edom . . .," warned Yahweh. The storm of God's wrath was coming closer. First the thunder was heard above the territory of faraway heathen nations unrelated to Israel: the Syrians, the Philistines, and the Phoenicians. The lightning destroyed the palaces of Damascus, Gaza and Tyre! But those cities were a comfortable distance away. In Samaria the people looked out the windows of their houses of ivory and said, "There's a bad storm over there, but fortunately it's far away." But the sky became darker as the storm came nearer. Amos then pronounced judgment on the Edomites, who were children of Esau, and the Ammonites and Moabites, who were children of Lot. Those nations were related to Israel by blood.

Look! The houses of Teman, Rabbah, and Kerioth are already going up in flames. It's getting too close for comfort. Don't you see it coming, you who are at ease in Jerusalem and secure in Samaria? The fire from heaven will strike you next!

That the prophet mentions Edom first when he turns to the three nations related to Israel should not surprise us, for he had already mentioned Edom's name twice in connection with the slave-trading of the Philistines and the Phoenicians. The Edomites were heavily involved in this business, for it was to them that the Israelite slaves were sold. They themselves had not yet been condemned, but now that Amos had finished with the Philistines and the Phoenicians, the Edomites got their turn. Amos would ultimately get around to all of them, for no sinner will escape destruction when God unleashes His wrath in judgment.

Edom's sin was not the same as Tyre's sin, which Amos had just dealt with. It was even worse! Amos accused Tyre of breach of contract and violating an agreement, but Edom's offense was a violation of blood ties. Edom was Jacob's brother in the flesh — they had been in their mother's womb together — while Solomon had only called Hiram his brother out of politeness. The violation of a bond based on a blood relationship stirred up the soul of the prophet. He couldn't get over it that Edom "pursued his *brother* with the sword, and *cast off all pity,* and his anger tore *perpetually.* "

O Esau, your tears were not genuine, and your grief was a sham. If your sorrow had been a *godly* sorrow, you would have been *reconciled* with your brother. But since your anger was perpetual and your wrath endless, it's crystal clear that your sorrow was a wordly sorrow. A sorrowful sinner can be angry *for a while,* but he cannot remain angry for the rest of his life. He may fall into sin, as Jacob can testify, but he cannot live in sin forever. Yet, that's just what Esau the Edomite did. His anger was never-ending.

It is striking that no particular offense of Edom is mentioned. While other nations were accused of specific atrocities, Edom was not. The prophet didn't even refer to Edom's slave-trading. The only thing said about Edom is that he is the *constant* enemy of his brother. Edom is accused of suppressing his natural feelings toward blood relations and perpetuating his enmity, refusing to be reconciled with his enemy. So stubborn was Edom in his anger and his unwillingness to forgive that the prophet Ezekiel later put his finger into the same wound when he declared on God's behalf: "Because Edom took deliberate revenge on Judah and by so doing incurred lasting guilt . . . " (Ezek. 25:12 NEB).

Do you understand what this means? it means that the sin of slave-trading is a trivial offense compared to the sin of irreconcilability. Enviousness and vindictiveness are much more serious sins than slave-trading. It will be easier on the day of judgment for the Syrians, who mutilated people by riding over them with threshing machines, and for the Philistines, who whipped their slaves savagely, than for a *brother* who keeps his anger forever!

Are you sure you understand what this means? Nothing arouses God's wrath more than brothers who quarrel and cannot get along together.

That should come as no surprise. God is love, and therefore nothing is more contrary to His nature and more certain to meet with His disapproval than hatred and enmity between brothers. God is a God of reconciliation, and therefore an irreconcilable spirit arouses His holy wrath.

Moreover, envy and anger are the root of *murder*. Nothing makes God more angry than murder, when a man raises his hand to strike down a bearer of God's own image. The punishment for this sin is terrible. "I will send a fire upon Teman, and it shall devour the strongholds of Bozrah" (1:12).

All of Edom, from Teman in the west to Bozrah in the east, will go up in flames, Amos prophesied. This is exactly what happened when bands of Assyrians plundered and burned in the hills of Edom, working their way from west to east.

Doesn't that seem typical of the Old Testament? Don't we sense something of a nationalistic wrath here? Doesn't the New Testament sing us a much more beautiful song of love? When we read in the Gospel that we are to *love* our enemies, don't we feel uneasy about Bozrah becoming a heap of rubble and our enemies being destroyed?

But listen once more to the words that come from the mouth of *love.* While God speaks of fire on the *earth,* Jesus speaks of the fires of *hell:* "But I say this to you: anyone who is angry with his brother will answer for it before the court; if a man calls his brother 'Fool' he will answer for it before the Sanhedrin; and if a man calls him 'Renegade' he will answer for it in hell fire" (Matt. 5:22 JB).

This enmity between Edom and Jacob was in essence the enmity between the world and the church, between the seed of the serpent and the seed of the woman, an enmity that originated in Paradise and continues throughout the ages. It revealed itself long ago in the struggle between Edom and Judah, and in the fullness of time it came into the open in the struggle between Herod and Jesus. It expanded in the history of the church and took on the form of a flame consuming the martyrs. In our time it is present in the struggle of godless Russian Communists against the church. One day it will reach its climax when the Antichrist appears. This perpetual wrath is the continuing antithesis. Once we realize this, we can understand why the enmity never ends. God Himself said in Paradise: "I will *put* enmity . . . ."

What cannot be explained or excused, however, is the enmity that is now at work dividing brothers from the same house gathered around the One we call the Prince of *Peace*. In the church we see divisions between brothers from one house — brothers who should live together in harmony. Just listen to quarrels and dissension in the homes of God's people. Look at the personal feuds between brothers and sisters.

Doesn't Amos sketch *our* sins accurately when he says, "He cast off all pity, and his anger tore perpetually"? Don't *we* need to repent and turn away from the greatest sin of Christianity and the churches in our time? Shouldn't *we* stop and think when we read that enmity is the greatest in the series of atrocities listed by God's prophet?

Don't be surprised if fire strikes our walls because of these sins, for Jesus speaks of the fires of hell. No, don't be surprised at all, for envy is already a fire; it is an unholy fire of discord. The fire of hell is that blazing, never to be extinguished, always spreading fire of the eternal quarrel that already flares up in our own hearts here on earth.

This punishment is the purest consequence of the deed. In our life on earth we already pay the price for this sin.

The first thing Amos says about Edom is that he has smothered all feelings of tenderness toward his brother. Then Amos declares that there is no end to Edom's anger. Finally he says that Edom keeps his enmity forever. This is the rational and inevitable climax of the irrationality of sin. Edom's sin begins by smothering all feelings of brotherhood and cutting the bonds between brothers. Once this has happened, anger is given free rein. And when things have gone that far, it is very difficult to hold anger in check, for the enmity continues. We may then say that all is forgiven, but nothing is really forgotten. Everything stays as it was. This is the sorrowful path of sin.

The unbending irreconcilability of Edom continues to this day and will continue until Christ returns. In the heart of the modern Temanite *hatred* lives on.

Yet the wrath that is bound to erupt sooner or later may slumber for some time. The wise Temanite likes to pretend he is an apostle of peace. His motto is: "Peace on earth." He wants nothing to do with "Glory to God" and does not speak of God's "good pleasure," but the "Peace on earth" of the Christmas story appeals to him as he hurls reproaches at the "church." Esau, not Jacob, is the peacemaker.

The wise Temanites of our age pose as apostles of peace. While they invent atom bombs in their wisdom, they also establish a United Nations Security Council. This false wisdom does not understand that as long as the root of murder remains untouched, "Peace on earth" will remain a fleeting dream. The prophetic statement that Edom's enmity is *perpetual* deeply disappoints the wise men of our age, so they deny it flatly.

The true wise man, who goes to Bethlehem, does not make threatening noises with weapons but envelops himself in the incense of prayer. Yet he does not claim to be better than anyone else. Jacob is just as sinful as Esau. His nature is also deeply corrupt, and there is enmity in the depths of his heart, too. Yet he knows of another peace. This peace of God presses him to make peace with his fellow man. It leaves him willing to be reconciled.

Thus the church should not look down on the world, just as Jacob should not think himself better than Esau. There is no reason for us to elevate ourselves. There is much more reason for us to be deeply ashamed of the fact that the church is still seething with enmity and petty quarrels.

Christ divides mankind into two camps, and this gives rise to two different kinds of wisdom, i.e., that of the Idumeans and that of the Israelites. Each one of us must ask himself on which side he stands. Anyone whose enmity *continues unabated* is on Esau's side.

Yet we do have reason to boast! The reason for our boasting lies not in ourselves but in the eternal good pleasure of which the angels also sang — the good pleasure that makes God say: "I have *loved* Jacob, but I have *hated* Esau."

6.
Sodom's
Poison

For three transgressions of the Ammonites . . .
(1:13).

The great sin that made God's judgment on the Ammonites irrevocable — to say nothing of the fact that there were four such known offenses — was that they had cut open pregnant women in Gilead. This atrocious practice was like the offense committed by the Syrians, who had ridden over the people of Gilead with threshing machines (1:3). Yes, the Syrians were guilty of the very offense the prophet Elisha had foreseen when he started weeping during a conversation with Hazael, their king (II Kings 8:12).

We should note that both the Syrians and the Ammonites committed these offenses against the inhabitants of *Gilead*, which was the battlefield of the Syrian wars. In II Samuel 10:6

we read about the Ammonites making common cause with the Syrians. Thus it appears that the historical event to which Amos here refers took place during the Syrian wars. It appears that the Ammonites, whether as allies of the Syrians or on their own, invaded Gilead and committed these offenses against its women during that era.

That Ammon did such a thing should surprise no one acquainted with history. These offenses were the effect of Sodom's poison, for Ammon had inherited sensual, almost sadistic tendencies.

Ammon was the second of the nations related to Israel by blood mentioned by Amos. Edom was the first. The Edomites were descendants of Esau, and thus were very close to Israel, while Ammon was the son of Lot's younger daughter.

Lot himself was the father of this child. We all know about the shameful events in the dark cave by Zoar that led to the birth of Ammon. It is a story stained and blemished by incest and drunkenness. That Lot's daughters could do such a thing shows how harmful his family's stay in Sodom had been.

No one can live in sin's neighborhood without being affected by it. These girls simply shook off any feelings of shame they might have had and cast aside any notions of morality. In Sodom the once virtuous girls had become insensitive to sin. Such is the background of Ammon's birth.

What would become of a child with such a mother, a child whose father was also his grandfather? One of God's ways of punishing the sins of fathers (as well as mothers) is that their children often turn out to be even greater sinners than the parents, engaging in sin that would make the parents blush in shame. This is exactly what happened in the case of the Ammonites, who seized pregnant women and cut them open. With wicked sensuality and sadistic enjoyment, they watched as the women writhed in pain and then died an agonizing death. Such sensual murder was fully in keeping with the wickedness of Sodom.

O Lot, what were you doing there with your daughters living in that city of sin?

The Ammonites were also in the grip of another kind of sensuality — the feeling of *power*. Amos points to this love of power as the chief motive behind their murders. The Ammonites wanted to *enlarge their borders* and expand their territory.

The drive to expand led to the most refined methods of waging war. Their war was not a defensive war or a war of liberation, nor were they seeking revenge for injustices they might have suffered earlier. Their military campaign was unadulterated imperialism.

Such wars are usually the most gruesome. The most terrible weapons are used to annihilate the enemy. Although bombs and machine guns were still unknown at that time, no one could deny that the Ammonites were thorough and methodical in their war of extermination, in their effort to take over Gilead by genocide. We, as twentieth century people, are also acquainted with such practices!

The Ammonites believed that the best way to attain their goal would be to leave no Israelite alive and kill even the *unborn children.*

> For three transgressions of the Ammonites,
> and for four, I will not revoke the punishment;
> because they have ripped up women with child in Gilead,
> that they might enlarge their border.

In this attempt to wipe out Israel's unborn generation, we see the savagery of the Ammonites against a much more important background. *Satan* was behind it. He tried to use the sensuality and wickedness of the Ammonites for a more significant goal of his own. That goal was to prevent the birth of the woman's Seed at all costs, for the birth of the Messiah would mean the crushing of his poisonous head. Therefore the promised One must not be born, reasoned satan, that murderer from the beginning. If only he could prevent it, he could expand his kingdom from sea to sea and from the rivers to the uttermost ends of the earth. Then he would not only be called the prince of this world but also the ruler of heaven.

Therefore he made a number of attempts to smother Israel's seed at birth. Through the Egyptian Pharaoh, satan commanded that all the male children of the Israelites be drowned in the Nile. Through Haman the Agagite, he commanded that all the Jews be eradicated.

The same ancient enemy of Christ was behind these Ammonites. To the children of Ammon, it seemed that the sensuality of the flesh and the love of power was driving them on. Yet, satan was using them in his attempt to prevent the birth of the Messiah.

Satan is not omniscient. Who could say whether one of those pregnant women might not be the one whom God had chosen to give birth to the Messiah? Who was to say whether those dying, unborn children might not include the dreaded Seed of the woman?

On the island of Patmos, John caught a prophetic glimpse of the war being waged throughout the ages, from Paradise to Paradise, when he wrote: "And the dragon stood before the woman who was about to bear a child, that he might devour her child when she brought it forth" (Rev. 12:4). That dragon, the old serpent, has always wanted to take the child away from the woman, and Christ away from the Church. And when that effort flounders, he tries to take the Church away from Christ. Thus the dragon stood before the woman about to give birth at the edge of the Nile. He confronted the woman when Susanna was put to the test. (Susanna's story is recorded in the Apocrypha.) He stood before the woman at the slaughter of the innocents in Bethlehem. And one day he will face the woman again when the Antichrist massacres the believers. Thus it was also the dragon who stood before the women in Gilead, seeking to devour their children, hoping to snatch *the* Child, the Son who is to rule all the nations with a rod of iron (Rev. 12:5).

When we look at the attacks of the Ammonites in Gilead in this light, the issue becomes painfully clear. Many things are clarified in the light of revelation. A barbarous atrocity once committed in the distant past in a little known place called Gilead becomes an assault on Christ. The inhabitants of Gilead and the children of Ammon fade away, and before our amazed eyes, Gilead, the battlefield of the Syrian wars, becomes a great battlefield in the struggle of all ages, a battlefield on which the heavenly throng and the armies of hell confront each other in a struggle for the world's great good and highest desire — the Child of Bethlehem, the Man on God's throne.

The dying mothers and wailing fathers were probably not aware that a clash between heaven and hell was taking place there in Gilead, just as we, unfortunately, are often unaware that a fierce battle is still being fought every moment — often right where we live. The battle is against *spiritual* wickedness in the air, while *we* are usually too busy with such tangible evils as pain and dying women to concern ourselves with spiritual wickedness "in the air"!

Thus there is a great deal to this story about the poor women in Gilead. First there is satan's attack on Jesus, God's holy Child. Then there is the feeling of power and the unbridled imperialism of the Ammonites. Finally there is the murder of defenseless women out of a sheer enjoyment of killing. Here we have three great offenses in one. Will the Judge of the entire earth remain silent? Can His judgment be escaped? Certainly not. The Lord declares:

> I will kindle a fire in the wall of Rabbah,
> and it shall devour her strongholds,
> with shouting in the day of battle,
> with a tempest in the day of the whirlwind;
> and their king shall go into exile,
> he and his princes together (1:14-15).

From the atrocities of the "barbaric" Ammonites to the "civilized" people of twentieth century Europe and North

America is only a small step, for the three great sins of Ammon can easily be found in our own time. The most widespread of them is the murder of *unborn children*. With flags flying and drums beating, this Ammonite practice has made a triumphant entry into many "civilized" nations and families — but with a difference. It is no longer called cruelty and murder — although some people are ashamed of it. Civilization has made such giant steps forward since the time of the Ammonites that all kinds of modern scientific tools have been invented, making it unnecessary to "cut open" pregnant women. A second step in this progressive direction is that murder is now called a sensible policy. After all, how am I to provide for a large family? How am I supposed to find room for so many children? We've certainly come a long way!

The second sin of the Ammonites was their anti-Christian raging against Christ. In our time we see this reflected most clearly in the godless things happening in Russia, the persecution that continues to surprise the supposedly "civilized" Western world that is itself engaged in murdering the coming generation. Yet this surprise will not last too long, for when the Antichrist takes control, many who are now appalled will join in willingly.

The third sin was the Ammonites' lust for power and their desire to expand, which led to the most cruel methods of warfare. I hardly need to remind you of what goes on in our time.

But what do you suppose God's response will be? Has God changed? Would the One who kindled a fire in the wall of Rabbah leave untouched the palaces of the power-seekers and the temples of the godless? Won't He have something to say to the people in our civilized era who insist that families must be limited to one or two children?

Let's not fall into the error of the Israelites of Amos's day. As they listened eagerly to the judgment preached against the heathens, they did not notice the storm getting closer and closer to them, for they were blind to *their own* sins.

Now, it's quite likely that you're not aware of having committed any sin like the sin of the Ammonites. Yet, you may be guilty all the same. If evil were solely a matter of some positive *deed,* a specific offense, there would be a good chance that you're not guilty. But you know — or you should know — that the negative sin of *omission* is just as great an evil in God's eyes. In one of the prayers in our liturgy, we confess that we have done what was forbidden and failed to do what we were commanded to do. Perhaps you like to distinguish between these two kinds of sin on the assumption that sins of commission are much worse than sins of omission. But the Lord doesn't make such distinctions. When the last judgment comes, those who have left all sorts of things *undone* — little things, we would say — will be banished to the outer darkness for *not* feeding the hungry, *not* visiting the prisoners, *not* clothing the naked. The failure to do these things testifies to a lack of love.

The offense of the Ammonites was enlarging their borders and stealing some of the territory of God's people. But some day the Lord will ask you, "What have you done to expand *My* territory?" Now, I know you have no positive transgressions like those of the Ammonites on your conscience. But what about your negative sins? Have you neglected to do what you should have done? Have you done everything you could to expand God's Kingdom? Do you sacrifice and pray and offer all your strength for this goal? That's your task! Or are you only concerned with your own territory? That's the question, and it must be taken seriously!

Amos tells us that the Ammonites will perish "with shouting in the day of battle, with a tempest in the day of the whirlwind." That's an Old Testament picture of what will happen before the last judgment. There will be battle cries, wars, rumors of wars, a storm like a whirlwind, and earthquakes in various places. In this tumult of war, this shaking of the foundations of the earth through all kinds of natural catastrophes, we hear the footsteps of the coming King. This King will send the king of the Ammonites and all his princes into exile.

Earthly kings will rise from their thrones in all their majesty and lay down their scepters. On their knees they will pay homage to the King whose Kingdom is not of this earth.

At midnight there was a cry: "The Bridegroom is coming! Let's go meet him." Are we ready?

7.
Burning Corpses and the Smell of Death

For three transgressions of Moab . . . (2:1).

The monotonous lament of Amos continues. He piles one judgment on top of another. Again and again we hear: "For three transgressions, and for four, I will not revoke the punishment." After Ammon, Moab, Lot's other son, gets his turn.

The storm raged on. Surely the lightning would strike Jerusalem before long. All the cities and palaces in the area around it were already in ruins, but the people of Jerusalem didn't sense what was coming.

Moab's offense was that "he burned to lime the bones of the king of Edom." This charge surprises us. We're used to Amos condemning heathen peoples, on God's behalf, for doing something to His covenant people. The victims may have been children of Judah, or children of Israel, or perhaps even children that have *deserted* Him — it makes no difference. The Lord becomes very angry when the heathens do anything to hurt *His* people.

But now we come to the sobering realization that the issue in the deepest sense was *not* His *people,* for it is apparent from God's complaint against Moab that He also takes the side of the *heathens.* Moab's offense was that he burned the bones of the king of *Edom.* In His amazing mercy the Lord raises His protective shield over the entire earth — not just over Judah and Israel, but even over Edom!

The more we read the Bible, the more God surprises us. Here we find Him actually taking *Edom's* side — the same Edom that Amos had just cursed because he pursued his brother with the sword! So definite was the Lord about this matter that Moab's sentence was irrevocable. Moab had committed an offense against Edom's king by violating his grave and his corpse.

What is behind the Lord's anger at this sin? The issue is not Israel or Edom but the *Lord Himself:* His own honor and holiness are at stake. It was not because Israel and Judah had shown themselves to be so worthy or because Edom's king was so highly thought of in heaven that Amos was commissioned to declare that God would punish those who had committed this offense against a human being.

In His anger at this transgression, the Lord was guarding His own glory. The attack on God's people made by Damascus and Tyre and others was ultimately an attack on God Himself. The apple of His eye had been cut open. Thus the offense which Moab committed against Edom's king in burning his corpse was also an offense against God. Although Edom was not part of God's *covenant people,* the Edomites were human beings all the same. They, too, were created in *God's image.* The burning of the king of Edom's bones until they turned to lime was an atrocity in God's eyes not because the king of Edom was a king but because he was a person created in God's image (and thus a *human* king). The holiness of this image in which man was created is even upheld by God outside the circles of His covenant people.

Biblical history does not include any account of the burning of the body of Edom's king. Yet there was one episode like it, which also involved Moab. In II Kings 3 we read that Mesha, the king of the Moabites, was besieged by an allied army made up of soldiers of the two Jehorams and the king of Edom. In this hour of peril, Mesha offered his first-born son, the young crown prince, as a flaming sacrifice on the wall.

Such gruesome human sacrifices were by no means unknown in the ancient Near East. Today, urns containing ashes are still being dug up at archeological sites under the foundations of houses and city gates. They represent building sacrifices intended to win the favor of some god, so that the city being built would be safe.

Mesha's intention was doubtless to win the favor of his god, who would then force the besieging army to withdraw. The army did withdraw — but not because of Mesha's god or the gruesome human sacrifice.

Yet this incident is not what Amos was referring to. The offense he meant was one like it — in fact, there were three or four of them. Amos says here that Moab burned the bones of Edom's king until they turned to lime, or dust. Some interpreters connect this text in Amos with II Kings 3, the passage mentioned above. According to them, Moab, angry at Edom because the siege had cost Mesha his son and the heir to his throne, later violated the grave of the king of Edom responsible for this siege and burned his bones. This would make Moab's offense even worse: burning a corpse together with violating a grave would be the worst conceivable offense in the ancient Near East.

In many passages the Bible expresses its abhorrence of the great evil of burning corpses. Not only does Amos condemn Moab to death for it, the prophet Isaiah regards it as a horrible curse as well (Is. 33:12). In the time of the first Jeroboam, another prophet from Judah could proclaim no greater horror against the altar at Bethel than to say that *human bones* would be burned on it. He named Josiah as the one who was to carry out this terrible curse of the Lord, which Josiah did obediently but with great reluctance (I Kings 13:2 and II Kings 23:20).

I don't suppose there are many Christians who want their bones burned until they turn to lime. Moreover, Christians abstain from such offensive practices as burning the bones of their enemies. Yet, there is an offense just as bad, and perhaps even worse, in Christian circles. That's becoming a *corpse* yourself, being so dead spiritually that you pollute the air around you with the smell of death, until the stench rises to heaven, where God is disgusted by it. Burning bones until they turn to lime is a serious matter, but it's much more serious for the church of the Lord to look like a field full of dead, dry bones that aren't even worth burning. When that happens, the smell of death pervades every nook and cranny. Why don't we live in fear of that smell?

It's striking that we are aware of the danger of committing major, positive sins but that the negative sin of omission no longer seems to burden our consciences. We think it's wrong to burn the bodies of the dead, but we take a certain pleasure in inhaling the smell of death. When heathen practices are revived in our time or when someone goes too far and does something horrible, we all deplore it, but we are hardly concerned about the fact that many of us are dead trees in God's garden, bearing no fruit to His glory.

God punishes sins of *omission* just as severely as sins of *commission*. He hates the smell of death just as much as He hates burning corpses. This is His judgment on Moab, who violated the bodies of the dead: "Moab shall die amid uproar, amid shouting and the sound of the trumpet" (2:2). Now listen to His judgment on those who are spiritually dead, on the fig tree that bears no fruit: "Cut it down. Why should it go on using up the soil?" (Luke 13:7 NEB).

The striking thing about the judgment on Moab is that Moab was to die amid *uproar*. This is significant especially in view of the fact that Jeremiah characterizes the Moabites as "sons of tumult" (Jer. 48:45), which leads us to suppose that they were known for their boisterousness. The people who were so boisterous in life would die amid hubbub and shouting. These children of tumult would perish in the tumult of war. Doesn't that seem fitting?

There's profound truth in this, and it doesn't apply to Moab only. A man will indeed die as he lived. We say of a rich man that his funeral was a fitting and worthy conclusion to his life. His life was filled with beauty and abundance, and so was his burial. We remember many of the details of his funeral service. But when a poor man like Lazarus dies, this is not the case. We simply say that he died. His funeral isn't worth talking about. We don't make much of the poor man after his death, for his life was as uneventful as his death. The Lazarus of Jesus' parable spent his days staring at the beautiful door of the rich man's house. He died just as he had lived — and the angels came and carried him to Abraham's bosom. Yet the angels did not make a big ceremony of it, either.

Today there are many people who die amid tumult. They are people who also make a lot of spiritual noise. There are beautiful automobiles and lengthy eulogies at their funerals. There's a great deal of sobbing and noise as everyone hears what great services the deceased has performed for church, state and society. Yet many of the people who make a lot of spiritual noise die in anxiety and darkness and fear of death.

There are also quiet people who pass on in peace with a psalm on their dry lips as they see lights burning in the many rooms of their Father's mansion. Just as they were still in life, so their death is peaceful.

Indeed, many a man dies just as he has lived. Let us pray that our death will not take place amid tumult, and that there will not be too many speeches at our funeral. For me, to live is Christ and to die is gain. That's the greatest comfort of all.

8.
Covenant
Breaking

For three transgressions of Judah . . . (2:4).

When Amos turned to Judah, he still had not reached his main goal, which was Israel. The task which Yahweh had given him was to pronounce God's judgment on the fallen kingdom of the ten tribes. He did so in such a way that every Israelite in Samaria could not help but realize that the message was ultimately meant for him.

The storm got closer and closer, as we have seen. It started in faraway heathen lands and then moved on to Edom, Ammon and Moab, which were heathen nations closely related to Israel. Now is was Judah's turn. Like Israel, Judah belonged to the *covenant people*.

There are good reasons why the prophet addressed himself to Judah before proclaiming his main message to Israel. First of all, as a prophet from Judah, Amos wanted to avoid any appearance of partiality. If he had said nothing about his own people but threatened the kingdom of the ten tribes with God's wrath, his hearers might have taken this as an excuse to simply cast his prophecy aside or consider it mere opinion. Therefore he could not afford to skip Judah.

In the second place, the judgment on Judah was a final effort to put the fear of the Lord into those who were at ease on the mountain of Samaria. Now that God's lightning was even consuming the palaces of *Jerusalem,* it was inconceivable that Samaria would be spared unless the people there repented.

But in the third place, the sins of Jerusalem had indeed become so great that one atrocity would make judgment irrevocable.

Just what was Judah's sin? The interesting thing is that the prophet doesn't tell us specifically. He speaks in generalities. He says nothing about burning the bodies of the dead, nor does he accuse his countrymen of murder or theft. Apparently none of the atrocities of which the heathens stood accused could be laid at Judah's doorstep.

The reason why Jerusalem's palaces were to be destroyed was *merely* that their inhabitants "have rejected the law of the Lord, and have not kept his statutes" (2:4). "Is that all?" you ask. Isn't that enough? That was the worst and most frightful thing they could do! That was covenant breaking! Everything else was subordinated to the great sin of covenant breaking!

It may well be that Judah refrained from the gruesome offenses of the heathens and to that extent lived a respectable life. Yet the simple fact that it did not keep God's "statutes" made it all the more detestable and ripe for judgment in the eyes of Yahweh.

Judah, of all nations, was God's covenant people. Judah was in a privileged position:

To Jacob he makes his word known,
his statutes and decrees to Israel;
he has not done this for any other nation,
nor taught them his decrees (Ps. 147:19-20 NEB).

Because God had done so much for Judah, its violation of
his law counted double. Therefore there was no *need* for
Amos to mention any particular offenses. Covenant breaking
was already serious enough.

Let's think about what this means for us! We have no
right to get excited about the excesses of the "evil" world
when we ourselves make fun of the "statutes of the Lord."
In fact, our behavior is twice as reprehensible. Those who
know what path to take but fail to take it will be punished
severely. When I speak of "making fun" of the Lord's statutes, I'm not exaggerating.

Let's take a look at the accusation made by Amos, in
the name of the Lord. Remember that what he said to Judah
is also meant for us! When we consider the accusation carefully, we see that it is not as vague and general as it might
appear at first. On the contrary, the sins of Judah are spelled
out in an unequivocal, specific way. Amos declares that
Judah is to be punished "because they have rejected the *law*
of the Lord, and have not kept his *statutes.*" We should note
that this is a double specification of Judah's transgressions.

In the first part of this accusation, Amos talks about the
"law," which is made up of the "statutes" mentioned in
the second part. The "law," the torah, is more general. The
"statutes" are more particular: they are the specific rules
and commandments. Thus Amos moves from the general to
the particular by explaining that "rejecting the *law* of the
Lord" simply means "not keeping His *statutes.*"

This is the part meant for us. As long as things are put
in general terms, we feel fairly safe. When the "law" is read
aloud in church, it does not frighten us. That's because we
refuse to move to the level of *specific* commandments or

"statutes." But we should take the time to ponder these statutes once, remembering that the commandment "Thou shalt not steal" means — among other things — that I must "do whatever I can for my neighbor's good" (*Heidelberg Catechism,* Answer 111). And we should apply the ninth commandment by reminding ourselves that we must "never give false testimony against anyone, twist no one's words, not gossip or slander, nor join in condemning anyone without a hearing or without a just cause" (Answer 112). We should go through the entire law and consider each statute in this way.

Any congregation that does so is likely to receive a healthy shock. We now see that the reason we're willing to go along with the law is that we don't take the particular "statutes" too seriously. Therefore, says Yahweh, "I will send a fire upon Judah, and it shall devour the strongholds of Jerusalem" (2:5).

Amos gives us a second specification when he equates *"rejecting* the law of the Lord" with *"not keeping* His statutes." Just as the "law" takes on concrete form in the "statutes," "rejecting" the law means "not keeping" the statutes. In short, when we fail to keep the law, we have rejected it.

We could put this point in different words by saying that "not doing something" (the negative side) can be just as sinful as a specific misdeed (the positive side). Sins of *omission* are no less terrible than sins of *commission.*

When we read through the Scriptures, we see this truth expressed in many different ways. Yet we like to think that sins of omission are less serious than sins of commission. When someone publicly "rejects" God's law and sins openly, we denounce him, but when someone fails to do what he should have done, such as seeking to honor God, loving his brother, or protecting his neighbor's reputation, we are still happy to consider him a friend and may even give him a place of honor.

Those sinners by omission, who "have not kept the

Lord's statutes," show that they are lacking in love, for love never leaves things undone but is always busy. In this light we see that the severe judgment on the sinners by omission, the sinners who *fail* to feed the hungry, is fair. They are lacking in love.

When we consider how seriously God takes these sins of omission, we realize what the judgment of the Lord, which we hear from the mouth of Amos, really means. God is saying, "Because they have *not* kept My statutes, I will send a fire upon Judah." Although no flagrant offense is mentioned, and although Amos speaks "only" of their "rejection" of the Lord's law and statutes, Judah's situation certainly looks grim. The complaint of Amos "hits home."

Amos does mention one specific statute of the torah: "They have been led astray by the false gods that their fathers followed" (2:4 NEB). Here it looks as though the complaint against Judah has become a complaint against certain false gods. This poetic and prophetic way of putting the point is certainly beautiful. In this statement we hear a kind of divine pain, a jealousy: the false gods have led *His* people astray.

Yes, the people of Judah certainly did go astray. And although idolatry had already caused their fathers untold misery, they continued in it. It was in their blood! In some places in the Bible we read that the people of Judah followed gods that their fathers were not acquainted with, but this does not conflict with the complaint of Amos, for entirely new gods were indeed imported from time to time. The fathers, of course, would not be familiar with these new gods, but they did have a good deal of experience with idolatry as such.

We have seen that Amos does not list the transgressions of Judah. Yet, if he must mention some specific statute that has been disregarded and calls for God's judgment, he will start with the *first commandment*. He does not point first of all to sins against the second table of the law. Instead he turns to the first table.

We might be inclined to disagree here. It's striking how much we talk about sins against our *neighbor* without getting upset about sins against the first table of the law. Often there seems to be little feeling of guilt connected with sins against that first table. The sin against the second commandment, that of trying to worship and serve God in some other way than He has commanded, is even "defended" by seemingly pious people. Man-made religions, in which people don't care to be asked to which *church* they belong, are regarded by many as the highest form of genuine religion. Therefore it's a good thing that Amos reminds us here that the Lord will send a fire upon Judah because of its sin against the *first and great commandment*.

Things certainly looked dark for Judah. All Amos ever seemed to talk about was judgment. I said "seemed," for this prophet also knew what grace is. David's fallen house *will* be raised again, he declared (9:11). This makes us think immediately of Jesus, who is a descendant of David. Jesus is our peace. He did not reject the law: He kept the statutes faithfully. He died for you and me, for people who reject the law and fail to keep the statutes. Because of our sins, judgment descended upon Him. Fire enveloped the Man of sorrows.

Let us seek our peace in Him by accusing ourselves of rejecting the law. And may His Spirit come into our hearts, so that our thankfulness will lead us not to reject His law and not to forget His statutes. "If you are my friends," says Jesus, "you will do as I have commanded."

9.
The Little Man

For three transgressions of Israel . . . (2:6).

The prophet has finally reached his goal. All along, he was heading for Israel. The preceding judgments against the *heathens* were only a prelude, for Amos's special assignment was to deal with the people of Israel, in the name of the Lord. A mild reprimand would not suffice. In the rest of the book, the heathens are not addressed again.

The prophecy of judgment against Israel differs from the prophecy of judgment against the heathens in an interesting and important way. The difference is that the *catalogue of sins* is much longer and more detailed in the case of the covenant people. When Amos talks about the heathen nations, he mentions only one flagrant offense for which they deserve

God's judgment. But when he talks about Israel, the people of God, he goes into the smallest details and presents a thorough report on their transgressions. This prophet from Tekoa deals with all the surrounding heathen nations in a single chapter (Amos 1), but he devotes almost an entire chapter to Israel alone (Amos 2).

God is much stricter with His own children than with those who are outside the covenant. He keeps a much closer eye on them than on the heathen nations. The sins of God's people count double.

Amos's preaching doubtless led to opposition from the Israelites. The people of Israel were accustomed to glorying in their position. They believed that because they were the "chosen people," God would never do anything to them but would always be on their side. This illusion was now torn to bits by Amos.

He agreed fully with the first part of Israel's reasoning. In the name of the Lord he proclaimed, "You only have I known of all the families of the earth." But he immediately went on to draw a different conclusion from this: "Therefore I will punish you for all your iniquities" (3:2). Hence, in the second chapter, he compiles an extensive and damning catalogue of Israel's sins.

God was not being unfair here. Because the Lord took care of Israel in a special, gracious way, He was justified in expecting much more from this favored nation. Nor was He being cruel. On the contrary, He revealed Himself here as an unchanging, faithful covenant God. If He had simply let everything go, He would have shown that He *did not* love His people, just as Eli's failure to be firm with his sons made him responsible for their downfall. Love *requires* that we be strict and firm.

God was motivated by His infinite love when He decided to investigate every nook and cranny of life in Israel, when He reprimanded His "chosen people" before all the nations, when He put a finger into an open wound, and when He caused His own people pain and threatened judgment. God in His love uses painful means to heal His loved ones and save them from corruption and sin.

Come, let us sing the praises of God's love, which is not too weak to take the trouble to be strict and firm. Let us be thankful for the detailed catalogue of sins that is read to us over Israel's head.

The citation from heaven reads as follows:

> For three transgressions of Israel,
> and for four, I will not revoke the punishment;
> because they sell the righteous for silver,
> and the needy for a pair of shoes —
> they that trample the head of the poor into the dust of the earth,
> and turn aside the way of the afflicted;
> a man and his father go in to the same maiden,
> so that my holy name is profaned;
> they lay themselves down beside every altar
> upon garments taken in pledge;
> and in the house of their God they drink
> the wine of those who have been fined (2:6-8).

Then follows a whole series of circumstances that make Israel's guilt even greater.

Two things stand out immediately in this summary of sins presented in the Word of God. We should give them our careful attention.

The first is that Amos does not mention only one transgression, as he had done in earlier cases: he gives us all four of them. Furthermore, all these transgressions, as we shall see, boil down to the same thing: the *oppression of the little man,* a loveless attitude toward the poor and weak in society.

Among the sins of which we sometimes repent, this one is usually *last* on the list — if, indeed, it appears at all. In this respect too, there's something wrong with us. A merciful attitude toward the poor and a willingness to assist them are not virtues that often stand out in the lives of God's otherwise upright people. Therefore we must get it through our thick skulls that Amos *began* his proclamation of judgment with this sin. It was because of this loveless attitude that God said:

> I will press you down in your place,
> as a cart full of sheaves presses down.
> Flight shall perish from the swift,
> and the strong shall not retain his strength,
> nor shall the mighty save his life (2:13-14).

The second thing we should note is that God always takes the side of the small and weak. When the powerful heathens committed their gruesome offenses, God took the side of His weak people Israel. Damascus and Gaza were condemned because they trampled on minorities. But when powerful people within the circle of the covenant started to assert themselves and trampled weaker brothers underfoot, God again chose the side of the little man — this time *within* Israel. Our *merciful* God gets very angry at those who are *unmerciful.*

He does not, however, take the side of the little man because the poor are always such fine and virtuous people. There are also rascals and deceivers among the poor. The Word of God is miles away from the type of socialism that would have you believe all the rich are crooks while all the poor are virtuous, and that the rich man winds up in hell *because* he was rich while Lazarus goes to heaven *because* he was poor.

No, that's not the way things work. In the final analysis, the Lord God asks us to be merciful not for the sake of the poor but for His own sake. Everything He does and demands is for His own sake. By being merciful, God's people are to celebrate the virtues of their merciful Father. They are to manifest His image. If they fail to do this, they are degenerate children. God has no more room for such people on earth than in heaven.

As we read further in Israel's catalogue of sins, our faces grow red with shame. The first sin is that they "sell the righteous for silver.'' The condition of the ''chosen people'' was indeed pitiful. The judges, who were called in God's name to see that justice was done, accepted *bribes* and condemned the innocent. This is what is meant by ''selling the righteous for silver.'' Israel's judges could be bought. Its judicial system discriminated against one class in favor of another. This was Israel's sin in the area of *law*.

Closely connected with it was the social injustice that ravaged the lives of many people: ''and they sell the needy for a pair of shoes.'' It was a law in Israel (Lev. 25:39, 47) that someone who was poor and could not pay off a certain debt must be allowed to work off the debt in manual labor by serving the person to whom he owed the money as a servant or slave, provided that the creditor was also an Israelite. This service was not to continue beyond the year of Jubilee, a provision that protected the rights of the poor on all sides.

In the days of Amos, this law was bent to such an extent — although the offenders claimed to be abiding by the letter of the law — that a needy person would be sold into slavery ''for a pair of shoes.'' In other words, the rich even had the poor work for them as slaves if they owed some trifling sum like the price of a pair of shoes.

The intent of the rich was not so much to get their own lawful property back as to build a society in which they, as ''capitalists,'' would be able to control the ''proletariat'' and the paupers. *They,* the rich, would take over the land acre by acre. The small land owners would lose their land and be made fully dependent.

Things must have been pretty bad for Amos to have to say that they ''trample the head of the poor into the dust of the earth.'' Having dust on one's head was a sign of mourning. The powerful were not satisfied until the wretched poor were completely cast down and plunged into sorrow.

The rich man lived a life of splendor and luxury, surrounded by beauty, while Lazarus lay before his decorated door, full of sores! That was Israel's social sin.

The third sin of which Amos accused the people lay in the area of morality, but it, too, was intimately connected with the two preceding sins. Again it involved doing as you please with the poor. Morality had sunk to such a level in Israel that "a man and his father go in to the same maiden." Immorality was so rampant that a son who sought out a young woman for sinful purposes would encounter his father, who had come to the woman for the same reason. What decadence!

The picture looks even worse when it becomes apparent that the young maiden referred to is a domestic servant. Domestic servants were also among the "poor." Their position in the household was one of dependence on the master and his sons. The powerful master and his sons then abused this situation and took advantage of defenseless servant girls.

These powerful masters "push the poor out of their path," as Amos puts it (2:7 JB). In the process, they push the poor right off the path of righteousness and rob them of their honor. And on the sabbath day we find these hypocrites sitting by "God's altars," singing the songs of Zion!

And that, finally, is the worst sin of all! That the judges do wrong and the capitalists abuse their power is bad enough, but the prophet's greatest contempt and indignation is reserved for a fourth sin:

> They lay themselves down *beside every altar*
> upon garments taken in pledge;
> and *in the house of their God* they drink
> the wine of those who have been fined.

Pay particular attention to the words I have italicized: beside *every* altar, in the *house of their God*. Thus we would not be justified in saying that these Israelites were pure hypocrites who sinned under cover of darkness but were always careful to behave properly in the "house of the Lord," for what they did in God's house was also scandalous.

They reclined on "garments taken in pledge." While

God had expressly commanded that a garment taken in pledge was to be returned before the sun went down (Ex. 22:26), explaining that He is "compassionate," the covenant people were so sinful that they did not take this commandment seriously, but appropriated these garments as their own property and lay down on them beside the altars.

In addition, they drank the wine of those who had been fined. The poor wine makers who were short of money often paid their penalties in produce. The judges and the powerful simply drank this wine "in the house of their God." What decadence!

When we hear all these things, we say, "What a horribly corrupt era!" And so it was. But if you would open your eyes once — really open them wide — and look around in *our* places of worship and beside *our* altars, you would find the same kind of spectacle.

When I look around in my church, I see someone sitting near me who forced his "brother" into bankruptcy so he could get his hands on some small sum he had lent the poor man. Over there is someone who is quick to send officers of the law to repossess a debtor's goods before the debtor has a fair chance to pay for them. Next to him sits someone who ignores government regulations on wages and prices, and in the front pew sits a man who doesn't pay his bills if he can get away with it.

All around me I see people who live in luxury stretched out next to the altar on "garments taken in pledge" as they drink the wine of those who have been fined — even if they call it communion wine. They sing that the swallow and the sparrow make their nests by God's altars, but they forget that they have feathered their own nests in a shameful way by relying on trickery and deceit. There they sit, right in the front pew!

I'm afraid that someone who reads this might still wash his hands and proclaim himself innocent, saying, "What evil people there are in the world and the church!" Therefore I must go further in probing their consciences.

Trampling the little man underfoot in Israel was a sin against the eighth commandment. It was theft! What does God require of us in the eighth commandment? "That I do whatever I can for my neighbor's good, that I treat him as I would like others to treat me, and that I work faithfully so that I may share with those in need" (*Heidelberg Catechism,* Answer 111).

As long as I interpret this to mean that I must do whatever I can for *my own* good and work faithfully to increase *my own* bank balance, I am a thief and an oppressor of the needy, for then I am *not* manifesting the image of my merciful Father. Then I am lying on garments taken in pledge and drinking the wine of those who have been fined!

The church of the Lord must be on guard, for the house of God is overflowing with such "offenders"! What brings the wrath of God upon my head is not theft in the ordinary sense but my *failure* to further my neighbor's welfare, my *failure* to deal with him as I would like others to deal with me, my *failure* to assist the needy when they cry out for help.

We close our hearts and our wallets when the poor ask for our help. We refuse to come to the telephone when the needy call, or we send them to someone else. We are not ready to step in when we see others suffering privation. We refuse to treat the poor as we would want to be treated if we were poor. We worry only about our own interests and welfare. Therefore, when we confess in church that God is truly good to Israel, after we have turned away someone in need the evening before, leaving him to starve to death, God will close His ears to our singing. He wants nothing to do with such unmerciful people.

The church of the Lord must be on guard!

We can certainly come up with plenty of "reasons" to justify our lack of sacrificial love and our self-centeredness. We argue that the money is wasted on that particular man, for he's not to be trusted, or that we have a hard enough time just looking after ourselves. One of our favorite ways of hiding our egoism is by passing our personal responsibility on to the community. Isn't the government supposed to look after those unfortunate souls? Can't the church do something?

Yes, things have gone so far in our well-ordered, thoroughly organized churches that we *trade in* our general office as believers, which of course is primary, for some particular office within the church. There's hardly anyone who remembers that each of us personally holds an office that includes the priestly function of mercy.

In theory we still confess that we are part of the *militant* church, but in reality we are at rest. We have heard a hundred sermons or more on sacrificial love, and sometimes we enjoy listening to them, but we do nothing about putting what we hear into practice. We continue to plod along, contented and self-satisfied. We discuss all sorts of important topics. We debate and hold long meetings. Yet the fire of love burns almost nowhere, and the general office of all believers withers. No one is left with the impression that we are merciful priests of a merciful God, helping the needy and promoting the *welfare* of our neighbors.

Then one day we are rudely awakened by the powerful Word of God, as we lie there on our garments taken in pledge! Let's hope that we wake up in time! Otherwise we may go right on sleeping until Jesus says, "I was hungry, and you gave Me no food. I never knew you."

O merciful God, use the sharp sword of Your powerful Word to make Your church merciful, just as You are merciful Yourself. Have pity on us and on our children!

10.
You and Me

Yet I . . . (2:9).
But you . . . (2:12).

The list of Israel's sins recited by the prophet was long and dreary. No doubt the prosecutor would demand a very severe sentence.

Why don't you shut up, Amos, before the Lord destroys us all in His wrath? His fury alone is enough to terrify us!

But Amos refused to shut up. He went on to say even more frightening things. The subject he turned to next was God's *love.*

Is that so frightening? It is, and it isn't. It's not frightening when the sunshine of God's love softens us and His mercy leads us to repentance, when the words "Truly God is good to Israel" issue from our trembling lips.

But love also needs to be put to the test. And when the love of God awakens no response in us, we certainly have reason to tremble. That love then becomes an intense glow, a scorching flame that consumes everything around it.

Listen to Amos's choice of words. By deliberately using the word *I* at the beginning of several sentences, the prophet of the Lord reminds the people how God gave fully of His love to pamper and favor Israel.

> I destroyed the Amorite before them (2:9).
> I brought you up out of the land of Egypt (2:10).
> I raised up some of your sons for prophets,
> and some of your young men for Nazirites (2:11).

We could hardly expect God to do more for Israel. He certainly didn't deal that way with other nations, which had to get along without His counsel and the benefits of His covenant.

Unfortunately, the result of these favors was not repentance and conversion but a growing opposition:

> You made the Nazirites drink wine,
> and commanded the prophets,
> saying, "You shall not prophesy" (2:12).

Amos is talking about a relationship between persons, between "you and me." The contrasts he draws are chilling and incomprehensible. Against the clear daylight of God's love, the dark night of Israel's sin looked even worse. Israel did not accept God's love gratefully but trampled on His feelings. God's love was *wounded,* and thus it stopped singing and started to roar instead. Who can contain his fear when he has heard the lion roar? When God's love has been spurned and cast aside, it is not safe to be near Him. We risk hell less by ignoring such great wrath than by ignoring such great love and generosity.

The best way for Amos, a messenger of God's judgment, to hurt the people of Israel was to tell them of God's love. The eyes of those accustomed to the darkness of night cannot bear the bright light of the noonday sun.

The list of benefits which the prophet read to Israel was long and impressive. When someone begins to sum up the Lord's mercies in his life, he does not quickly reach the end. They are as numerous as the grains of sand on the seashore and can never be adequately pictured or described.

The list of benefits contrasted sharply with Israel's catalogue of sins. In the light of these mercies, Israel's sin was all the more inexcusable.

First Amos tells us some of the things God did for Israel:

> It was I who overthrew the Amorites when they attacked,
> men tall as cedars and strong as oaks,
> I who destroyed them,
> both fruit above ground
> and root below (2:9 JB).

Yes, God had indeed been good to Israel. The size of the giants who inhabited Canaan was no problem to Him. He eradicated them root and branch. He destroyed them so His people could take possession of the good and beautiful land He had promised them.

Before a single arrow was released, the powerful fortress of Jericho fell. *I* did that, O Israel! Your good fortune was the result *not* of *your* wisdom but of *My* blessing. The covenant you entered into, the heavenly Canaan that was promised you, is something *you* asked for but *I* gave you.

Amos continues with what God did for Israel:

> It was I who brought you out of the land of Egypt
> and for forty years led you through the wilderness
> to take possession of the Amorite's country (2:10 JB).

These are also words to ponder carefully, words of great value and comfort.

Did it perhaps occur to you that the prophet might have been better off leaving out this particular "proof of God's mercy"? Isn't there something strange about speaking of the forty years in the wilderness as a *favor?* Wasn't the period in the desert more of a punishment than a blessing? That's how it looks to us!

To us it seems that the forty years in the wilderness must have been one of the darkest periods in Israel's national life. Israel then led a nomadic life, without land and without rest. The Israelites perished under the sun's extreme heat and the plagues sent by God. They had to survive under the watchful eye of hostile tribes. The exodus from Egypt was certainly a step in the right direction, but weren't those forty years a dark chapter in Israel's history? Then why does the prophet speak of those dark years as a blessing?

After forty years, this band of weaklings that knew only how to make bricks appeared as a well-equipped army before the gates of the frightened Canaanites. This was *the Lord's* doing. Amos tells us that the *purpose* of those forty years was "to take possession of the Amorite's country."

A little earlier, you may have been taken aback when I spoke of the benefits that rain down on us from God's hand. Perhaps you looked at your own life and decided it was not much more than a journey through the wilderness, full of disappointments, sorrow and bitterness. Maybe you've suffered thirty or forty or even fifty years of pain and disappointment! But consider how all affliction counts as blessing in heaven's eyes. God put you through so much hardship not to torment you — as it sometimes seems — but to sanctify you and prepare you for your inheritance, to get you ready to "take possession of the Amorite's country." Without this preparation, you simply won't be ready for life on the new earth.

Isn't the beauty and goodness of the New Jerusalem a great enough gain to offset what you have lost here on earth? Can't you spare forty years for that?

Now comes the third benefit. God intended the Israelites to inherit the *land* of the Canaanites, but He did not want them to become heirs of the Canaanite *spirit*. Therefore He gave them everything they needed to avoid this evil. During the forty years in the wilderness, He not only prepared His people to be strong in warfare but also equipped them with spiritual weapons to overcome the spiritual evils of Canaan. In other words, He gave them His law.

Later He sent Israel men whose task it was to combat those evil influences. The prophets did so through their *words* and the Nazirites through their *example*. The outward appearance of the Nazirites was a reminder of the holy covenant between God and Israel. The prophets testified to this same covenant in their own fiery way. Both the Nazirites and the prophets combatted the spirit of the times constantly; both tried to build a spiritual wall around Israel. They declared that Israel's strength lay in its isolation. That's the background to the words: "And I raised up some of your sons for prophets, and some of your young men for Nazirites" (2:11).

I will not make any attempt to apply this to our time. I do not dare raise the question whether God has smothered His church with material and spiritual proofs of His favor. Instead I will use the words of the prophet to appeal to your consciences: "Is it not indeed so, O people of Israel?" (2:11).

It is noteworthy that after Amos reminded the Israelites of all the things God had done for them, he did not repeat Israel's sins. Those sins are well known to us. Despite the wall built by the Nazirites and the prophets, Israel did absorb the Canaanite spirit. It forgot that, as a theocratic people, it was supposed to reflect the image of a merciful God. Like heathens, the Israelites pushed the poor out of their path and sold the needy for the price of a pair of shoes.

But at this point, the prophet is silent about all those sins. By way of contrast, he now puts his finger into a much more serious wound. He points to a sin much worse than all the flagrant offenses summed up in 2:6-8, a sin even worse than the atrocities committed by the heathen nations condemned earlier. Israel's wickedness and hardness of heart reached a climax in this sin. What was this sin?

Much worse than drinking the wine of those who had

been fined or lying on garments taken in pledge was "making the Nazirites drink wine." Much worse than plunging the poor into sorrow and misery or raping a servant girl was saying to the prophets, "You shall not prophesy" (2:12).

At first glance the earlier offenses seem much more serious than whatever must lie behind this strange talk of giving wine to the Nazirites and forbidding the prophets to speak. One might argue that God must have intended us to drink the wine He made, and that limits on how long prophets may speak are a good idea, for otherwise we would get tired of listening to them.

Someone whose ears and heart are closed to "prophecy," who is deaf to God's Word, who is irregular in church attendance, may not have nearly as bad a reputation as an unfeeling person or an adulterer. But the Bible does not look at these things in the same way we do. Let's try to figure out why.

What Israel did was certainly *understandable.* The Nazirites and the prophets came to shake those who were "at ease in Zion" out of their peaceful lives of sin. They appealed continually to the consciences of the people. The Israelites did not like being reminded of their sins all the time. When the Nazirites and prophets persisted, the pangs of conscience eventually became intolerable. Therefore the Israelites began to resent the prophets. In time they came to hate those bearers of the truth, who had once enjoyed greater prestige and recognition among them than heroes and artists did among heathen peoples. The only way to put an end to the unrest, people thought, was to silence the voice of reproach. The voice of the prophets could not be silenced by argument: truth can never be silenced this way. Consequently a more radical approach was adopted. The prophets were forbidden to speak.

Such an approach testifies to *weakness.* The weakness of the person who has no grounds for his position manifests itself in the brutality of the command to be silent. A dictator, for example, muzzles the press when he is displeased with what it says. Anyone against whom he cannot hold his own in an argument is silenced.

There is also a more cunning way of resolving the problem. The devil often resorts to cunning when other methods fail. Thus he encouraged the people to give the Nazirites wine to drink. Once they were drunk, they would be open to his suggestions. Every dictator knows how to silence his opponent by getting him drunk, for once he's drunk he can be induced to sing the dictator's praises. This was the method Israel turned to. It was a grievous sin.

The spiritual decline of Israel was not apparent from its attitude toward outward ceremonies. Dr. B. Wielenga writes:

> The forms were left untouched, for ceremony is slow to affect the conscience. Yet, all that testified to the truth in a more direct way came to be hated. The self-denial of the Nazirites and the heroic stature of the prophets tormented consciences. Therefore people tried to silence these voices. The most ungodly thing of all happened: Israel struggled against God in the most intimate aspect of His revelation. It rejected the most tender gift of His covenant love. This was a scandal without parallel in history, which was to be outdone only by the murder on the cross. Israel rejected Jesus when it said, "You shall not prophesy."

There are many people in the churches who resist the Word of God. They do so neither by slamming the door in the face of elders or ministers who call on them nor by avoiding worship services. On the contrary, they cling to these forms with painful tenacity. Apparently, resisting the Word does not disturb their consciences.

Even less would these people consider doing away with the "prophets" in some brutal way or getting the "Nazirites" drunk. Many of them attend meetings to protest religious persecution and declare in song that God's Word abides forever and will not change in the slightest. Solemnly they sing that satan has reason to tremble, but they forget that they, too, have reason to tremble, since they — like the devil — continually resist the Word in their hearts.

While the Word tells us to love our brothers and think

in terms of forgiveness, these people continue to hold grudges year after year. Although the Word testifies that God loves a cheerful giver, miserliness traps them in her snares. Although the Word tells us to think of the Lord in all we do, they choose their own path through life.

Meanwhile they sing, "Blessed the people that listens to the Lord," thereby making it even worse for themselves. The murderer, the whore and the tax-collector will have an easier time of it than these silent opponents of the Word — unless the simple conversion story of Lydia becomes their story: "The *Lord* opened her heart to *give heed* to what was said by Paul" (Acts 16:14).

11.
The Creaking Wagon

Behold, I will press you down in your place,
as a cart full of sheaves presses down (2:13).

Now the Lord starts to *threaten* Israel. He says, "Behold,
I will . . . . " From His mouth come some terrible words
directed at His people.

The fearful thing is that the God who is willing to bring
so much *suffering* on His people is *the same God* who had
poured out so many blessings on Israel. The One who now
says, "I will . . ." is the same One who earlier complained

in wounded love, "I have destroyed the Amorite, and I brought you up out of the land of Egypt." But now we hear: "Behold, I will press you down in your place."

Did it have to come to this? God must have been aggravated for a long, long time before that inexhaustible patience was finally exhausted and His sun could no longer shine!

We must be very careful not to forget about the light and good will emanating from God's nature, for it was only after a whole series of blessings introduced by the words "I have . . ." that the threat finally came, introduced by the words "I will . . . ." This is indeed the inevitable outcome if we let all God's blessings roll off our backs like water off a duck's back.

The God of blessing now becomes a God of judgment. Yet, He is the same God. Health and sickness, rain and drought, prosperity and adversity, benefits and threats all have one and the same Author. In the deepest sense this Author is a *Father* — for all these things come to us not by chance but from His *fatherly* hand.

The judgment now threatened by God is: "I will press you down in your place, as a cart full of sheaves presses down." The meaning of this text is somewhat unclear; scholars have offered many conflicting interpretations of it. Yet, what it all boils down to is that there will be a "pressing," a judgment.

This was an entirely unexpected and unwelcome message for the Israelites — all the more because Amos declared that the catastrophe of which he spoke would occur on "that day" (2:16). There was no need to elaborate on this phrase, for everyone knew that it meant the day of Yahweh, the day of the Lord, the great day.

Israel had some very optimistic expectations about "that day." The Israelites had heard from Joel that it would mean ruin for the heathens but would bring salvation for God's people. The Israelites of the flesh, assured that they were "children of Abraham," forgot completely that

Abraham was the father of *believers,* and that the important thing is the *spiritual* bond with God.

Therefore the prophet Amos came to clarify Joel's prophecy by making it clear that it will be just as dark for unconverted Israelites on that day as for the heathens. The fire that will consume the palaces of the heathen cities will also burn those Israelites who loved the sins of the Canaanites and were completely at ease in Zion.

But in our text for this chapter, Amos was talking not about a fire that would destroy the homes of the Israelites but about a heavy wagon. Yet it amounted to the same thing.

The Israelites were not expecting such a message, nor did they believe it when they heard it. They were at ease!

"Behold, I will press you down in your place, as a cart full of sheaves presses down." There are a number of explanations of this text. It seems to me that we are to think here of a wagon used at harvest time. This wagon is so overloaded with sheaves that it creaks and grates. What the prophet was saying is that the Israelite state would start to look or sound like such a creaking wagon — even though the kingdom of Israel was enjoying exceptional prosperity under the second Jeroboam. The Israelites might have thought of the kingdom in the days when Amos prophesied as a brand-new streamlined automobile — although this would be something of an anachronism. Before long, however, they would compare the condition of the kingdom to an old, creaking, dilapidated farmer's wagon instead.

The "creaking" would be caused by the pressure of a burden — the burden of God's judgment. But the wagon would not creak forever: the creaking would be a prelude to its total collapse. When "that day" comes, people will stand weeping by the once-beautiful wagon of Israel, just as we gather tearfully around the wreckage of an automobile involved in a traffic accident.

Amos indicates the effect of the collapse by moving quickly from the image of the creaking wagon to that of an army that has been routed:

Flight will not save even the swift,
the strong man will find his strength useless,
the mighty man will be powerless to save himself.
The bowman will not stand his ground,
the fast runner will not escape,
the horseman will not save himself,
the bravest warriors will run away naked that day (2:14-16 JB).

Catastrophe! Total ruin!

When Amos *announced* the judgment, he thought of a creaking wagon making its last trip. When he *elaborated* on the judgment, he saw a defeated army in his prophetic eye. It is conceivable and not improbable that this man, in whose mind images succeeded one another so rapidly, was thinking of the earthquake in and through all of this! At the very beginning of his book, Amos reminded his readers that his words had been spoken "two years before the earthquake." The "creaking" also fits in with the image of the earthquake, for when the ground moves, walls and houses creak as they collapse. The words Amos uses to describe the catastrophe are also characteristic of an earthquake. When we read that neither the fast runner nor the strong man nor the bowman nor the horseman will escape, we think of war, but this would also fit in with an earthquake.

When God speaks to us through an earthquake, when all the powers of the creation fall with thundering force upon man, important people suddenly become small. Neither their *natural strength* nor what they have *learned* can protect them. Thus Amos speaks here of both nature and culture. The swift runner who can flee the deadly arrow in battle will not be able to run fast enough to escape the mountains and hills falling on him. The bold hero who would normally dare take on ten men at once will run away naked — but he will not escape! The *natural* power of the strong man will not save him from those falling mountains and rumbling hills! Neither will man's *cultural* accomplishments deliver him. The most primitive and basic elements of man's culture are mentioned here: the bow and arrow that man made so long ago and the horse he trained for his own use.

In our time, this primitive culture has advanced a long way toward perfection. But modern man, who builds towers and fortresses for himself, who conquers the depths of the sea with submarines and the atmosphere above the earth with airplanes, is hopelessly weak when God speaks. Just as God can turn the finest airplane into a wreck by uttering one Word, He will continue to intervene in the life of the strong man, to show him how weak he really is. Man, who prides himself on being the owner of luxurious vehicles that carry him as quick as lightning to the heights of enjoyment, is suddenly placed by God in a creaking wagon that will no longer advance and cannot be repaired even by the most capable "expert."

When God speaks, we hear creaking everywhere. Wise men are silent, and government leaders are perplexed. This is basically what Amos has to say to twentieth century man when he talks about the creaking wagon, the swift runner who will not escape, and the soldier whose bow and arrow will not protect him. This is how we must understand and apply these words from the distant past; otherwise they will leave us right where we are.

The Word of God is full of fresh perspectives. Behind the earthquake that is to come on "that day," the great and celebrated day of the Lord, *we* see the day of which Jesus spoke, the great day of His return, when the trumpet blows for the last time and the elements of the earth are consumed by fire.

The day of the Lord will certainly arrive unexpectedly, but its coming will not be without warning. We will be prepared for it by many "signs of the times." Anyone who knows how to read the signs of the times will be able to see the catastrophe of the creaking wagon approaching. Isn't the fact that the wagons are creaking an infallible "sign" that He will not wait much longer? Do you hear the wagon creaking?

You don't need especially good ears to hear the creaking and groaning and screaming and grating everywhere in the world. You don't need sharp eyes to see the wagon lurching from side to side in a dangerous way. Don't you see that the driver is in great peril? Only people who are completely deaf — such as those who are at ease in Zion — could continue to sing above all the grating sounds.

Is our wagon creaking? Don't you hear anything? Over there I see a marriage and family in which the foundations are so hopelessly rusty and weakened that a complete collapse can't possibly be far away. The wagon of our church life is not rolling along very smoothly either. We're short of oil — the oil of the Spirit! The church doesn't run like a well-oiled machine, even if it sometimes looks like one. Some people on the wagon are singing loudly, but God plugs His ears and cries out, "Stop! I can't bear to listen any longer to the grating sounds of your clamorous voices as you sing about Me." Thus, despite all the formalities we observe scrupulously, there is creaking to be heard everywhere.

Some people are already jumping off the wagon of the church, for they want to ride on the faster wagon of some "movement" — there is no "movement" in the church — and get to the goal more quickly.

We hear creaking in the home, grating sounds in the church, and rasping in our spiritual life. Those are all signs of the coming collapse, of the time when the Antichrist and his henchmen will be able to dance their devilish dance on the ruins of the church, the family and morality.

In social, political and international affairs, things aren't much better. We speak of the creaking in economic life as a "crisis." We devise strategies to "survive" the crisis; we try to "adapt" ourselves. We forget that the creaking is only a *sign* of what is to come. In various spheres of life it is already apparent that where there was once strength, there is only weakness now. Human courage is giving way to a feeling of hopelessness and helplessness.

The swift runners are standing still, and the soldiers aren't doing anything with their bows and arrows. Will they survive when the waters of the Jordan rise on "that day"?

In the oppressive anxiety caused by the creaking and near-collapse of Israel's wagon, there is still a small ray of hope, for the prophet Amos does not speak of just any wagon but of a *harvest* wagon completely loaded with sheaves. I cannot help but believe that this additional detail has a meaning of some sort. Nothing in the Scriptures is without meaning — not even the smallest detail. I do not believe that Amos used this image of the harvest wagon only because he was an outdoorsman well acquainted with the life of the farmer. Yet we must be careful not to read something into Scripture that isn't really there.

Whenever we speak of judgment, we may speak of light as well, for God is not only just but also merciful. I am intrigued by the fact that the wagon of which Amos speaks was a *harvest* wagon, and that this creaking harvest wagon was intended to bring the grain to the place where it is threshed, i.e., to some sort of barn. Without allegorizing about separating the wheat from the chaff, and without becoming curious about what happened to this wagon that carried such a precious but also frightening cargo, we may still say that God's creaking and judgment had a definite purpose, that He has taken the "remnant" to its destination.

"Behold, I will press you down in your place." He really will! But there are always some who are *not* killed, who do not perish under the crushing weight. Although the creaking is a miserable sound and the weight a dreadful burden, they are sanctified and purified by suffering, by bearing such a burden.

The creaking wagon is frightening. It means colossal ruin, and in this God's justice is glorified. Yet the sheaves on the wagon remind us that what God has made ripe in the field of this world will not be destroyed in judgment. And in this God's mercy is glorified.

Do you hear the creaking? Is there creaking in your life, too? Do you feel the pressure of God's heavy hand upon you?

You say that you do. Well then, are you familiar with the Psalms? If the weight of this burden does not crush you but sanctifies you instead, I believe you'll start reading the Psalms. Your prayer will be: "Let me not languish in my affliction." Your hope will be: "Long have I awaited the Lord in my affliction." Your song will be: "He will lighten the burdens of the afflicted." Your joy will be: "This is my comfort in my affliction."

I have another question for you: Do you know Jesus? The Bible says of Him that He was *oppressed* and even afflicted. There was a great deal of creaking in His life, which ended in a horrible death. Because He was oppressed and subjected to such horrible torment, because His life was full of grating and creaking sounds when everything fell apart for Him, we may share the psalmist's hope that the sheaves will eventually be brought into the barn with great rejoicing.

By keeping one eye fixed on the Savior, *spiritual* Israel can see a salutary and comforting side to the day of the Lord, the great and celebrated day when there will be much creaking. Joyfully the church proclaims: "In all my distress and persecution I turn my eyes to the heavens and confidently await as judge the very One who has already stood trial in my place before God and so has removed the whole curse from me. All his enemies and mine he will condemn to everlasting punishment: but me and all his chosen ones he will take along with him into the joy and the glory of heaven" (*Heidelberg Catechism,* Answer 52).

12.
Some Simple Questions

Do two men take the road together if they have not planned to do so?

Does the lion roar in the jungle if no prey has been found?

Does the young lion growl in his lair if he has captured nothing?

Does the bird fall to the ground if no trap has been set?

Does the snare spring up from the ground if nothing has been caught?

Does the trumpet sound in the city without the populace becoming alarmed? (3:3-6 JB).

We are foolish people who ask question after question. Answering these questions is often very difficult. We "struggle with the problem," as we like to put it.

In the third chapter of the book of Amos, we read a whole series of questions posed not by man but by God, questions that form our text for this chapter. The striking thing about these questions posed by God, who is so wise, is that they are so simple that even a child could answer them immediately. The problem God is struggling with is not the complexity of the questions themselves but why man cannot answer these childlike, simple questions — or why he doesn't *want* to answer them. This is something which amazes heaven.

The six questions that Amos poses here in God's name are all related and all have to do with the judgment announced against Israel. Yet each one has its own content.

God doesn't ask questions like a whining child who repeats the same request again and again. He asks questions like a skillful interrogator who probes deeper and deeper with each succeeding question.

The first question raises the issue whether the judgment announced is perhaps *unfair*. Israel certainly thought it was. Everyone in Israel agreed that God should punish the heathen nations, but the idea that the "chosen people" might be punished even more than the heathens led to universal protest. God had said: "You only have I known of all the families of the earth" (3:2). The conclusion the Israelites drew from this was: "Therefore I will send you only undisguised blessings." The Israelites regarded God in the same way that some people in our time like to think of Him, that is, as a rich uncle from whom one can expect an inheritance in dollars and cents. In the name of God, Amos said instead: "Therefore I will punish you for all your iniquities." This, the people thought, made no sense whatsoever. God would surely continue to favor Israel — at all times and under all circumstances. There was no need to expect judgment, for there was no reason for God to punish Israel.

To dispel this illusion, God asked a simple question: "Do two men travel together unless they have agreed?"

(3:3 NEB). Can a covenant endure if one of the parties regards the agreement as a mere scrap of paper? Is a contract binding if one of the parties violates the agreement? Can a marriage survive if one of the marriage partners is unfaithful? Can the Lord walk beside Israel if Israel refuses to walk beside the Lord?

What about it? Do two people travel together if they are not in agreement? That's hardly a riddle! Giving an answer is as simple as saying hello. A child could answer that question! But the Lord complains, "My people do not understand." The "chosen people" of the twentieth century, who moan and complain, who worry and ask why, who wonder what they are to think of God, would surely do well to reduce all their problems to this simple question that comes from heaven: "Do two men travel together unless they have agreed?"

The second question is equally simple: "Does a lion roar in the forest if he has no prey?" (3:4 NEB). This time the image is taken not from human society but from the world of animals. As the image changes, so does the *intention* of the questioner. This time the intention is not to show that there is a *reason* for the punishment but to indicate that the punishment is *irrevocable*.

In an almost monotonous way, the prophet had said again and again: "For three transgressions, and for four, I will *not revoke* the punishment." That, of course, met with even stronger denials in Israel. People thought the picture couldn't be as dark as Amos argued. Prophets are always such pessimists! Those who were at ease in Zion didn't tremble at what Amos prophesied. They laughed a bit and sipped their wine.

To the people in Samaria, who were laughing and making small talk, totally unaware of any danger, Amos addressed this question: "Does a lion roar in the forest if he has no prey?" Now, everyone knows that the lion does not begin to growl until he is ready to jump on his prey. The lion's roar is an indication that he is very close to his prey, that it's too late for escape. The lion is patient. Roaring too soon would alert his prey to the danger. The moment the lion roars is the moment when the defenseless victim is crushed and eaten.

Remember, Jerusalem and Samaria, the lion *has* roared! The Lord *has* arisen and left His holy dwelling place. Will anyone escape? The question is so simple that even a child could answer it. But the Lord complains, "My people do not understand."

The third question is even more ominous in its implications: "Does a young lion cry out from his den if he has taken nothing?" Here we do not see the lion about to attack his victim: we see him *devouring* his prey. Amos pictures the lion in his den, roaring in pleasure at his catch. Is escape still possible now? The question is simple. Even a child could answer it. But the Lord complains, "My people do not understand."

No, they really don't understand. There are many people today who, like those people in Samaria, bring their offerings and fold their hands in prayer without understanding that they are *dead* and have been dead a long time. Israel is not about to die: it is *already* dead. The lion is not about to eat: he has already been chewing on the carcass for some time. Forgetting this is one of the many mistakes made by "pious people" in our time.

From lions Amos now turns to birds. The abundance of the images succeeding one another rapidly forms a somber contrast with the death and gloom they portray. Amos's fourth question is: "Does a bird fall in a snare on the earth when there is no trap for it?" The snare mentioned here must be thought of as a net covered by two frames or screens that close quickly — just like a woman's purse — as soon as a bird falls into it. Such a snare would close automatically. The meaning of the second part of 3:5 is not that someone picks up the snare from the ground, for the snare springs up by itself. "Does a snare spring up from the ground," Amos asks, "when it has taken nothing?"

These two questions have roughly the same purpose as the two questions about lions. The lion will not roar until it is sure of its prey. The bird does not plunge to earth until it is sure of getting something to eat. The snare does not snap shut unless some foolish bird has ventured inside. In different keys and variations, Amos keeps making the same point: the judgment is irrevocable, and the punishment has already been decided.

Yet these questions about the bird and the bait used to trap it are by no means repetitious. Nothing in God's Word is without meaning — not even the apparent repetition of questions. God is like a relentless interrogator who probes deeper with each succeeding question.

The new element introduced by the questions about the bird and the net is the issue of *guilt*. We would not be justified in saying that the defenseless lamb becomes the lion's prey because of its own guilt, but the bird's downfall is definitely its own fault. It was the result of its own foolishness. The bird is attracted by the tasty bait and descends into the net. Thus this image involves an element not present in the example of the lion and its prey. Your death, Israel, is your own fault; it is the result of your own foolishness.

Here Amos is using prophetic *irony*. He compares Israel to a stupid bird. The bird sees a tempting piece of bait and goes after it. It eats the bait with great pleasure, but at the same time seals its death, for as it is calmly eating, the trap snaps shut. This is the bitter irony of heaven!

Jesus once raised the question whether man is superior to the birds of the heavens, and now we must give the humbling answer that man is indeed superior — in stupidity! How many stupid birds the human race contains! What birds do not know, man, who has the ability to trap birds, certainly should know!

We ought to be aware by now that if we feast on the delicacies of the world and revel in the service of sin and go after every piece of bait the devil dangles before us, we must first make sure that the world and its delicacies do not turn out to be a net intended to trap us. The wise people who bring about their own death by going after the bait outnumber the stupid birds caught in the snare. This text about the birds and the net reminds us of Paul's famous warning that when we sin, we become the *slaves* of sin.

"Does a snare spring up from the ground when it has taken nothing?" The question is simple. Even a child could answer it. But the Lord complains, "My people do not understand."

Finally the prophet asks: "Does the trumpet sound in the city without the populace becoming alarmed?" This question has a somewhat different meaning. First God asks whether there is good *reason* for judgment, for two people cannot travel together if they are not agreed. Then He asks whether the judgment is *irrevocable*. Now the issue is what the *effect* of the judgment will be. This is the most profound question of all.

God takes no pleasure in the death of sinners. Instead, He wants them to repent and live.

This sixth question indicates that all those prophecies of judgment were still conditional. God's hope was that the preaching would produce a healthy trembling in the nation, just as the people of a city are brought together in fear when the trumpet is blown to announce that the enemy is at the gates.

"Does the trumpet sound in the city without the populace becoming alarmed?" The question is simple. Even a child could answer it. But the Lord complains, "My people do not understand."

Now God considers the following problem: Although people everywhere are afraid of dying, Israel does not seem to be afraid. People jammed together in the city tremble in fear of death when they hear the trumpet, but Israel doesn't tremble. The Israelites laugh and sip their wine!

We, as human beings, ask questions. God asks questions, too. We pose very important and complicated questions for Him. He asks us some very simple questions. We ask so many questions that we can scarcely hear God's voice speaking to us above the clamor of our own voices.

We must learn to listen carefully to what God asks us, and we must learn to tremble — not because of the severity of the punishment but because of the greatness of God. We must learn to tremble at God's six questions; otherwise we will find ourselves unable to speak when He asks us a thousand questions for which we have no answers. We must learn to tremble when the trumpet is blown to sound the alarm and signal the coming judgment. Then we will also learn to rejoice at the sound of the gospel's trumpet.

God asks questions. He asks you and me, "Can't we travel together? Can't we be in agreement?" He asks, "Do all of you want to desert Me?" The question is simple and clear. A child — provided he is a child of God — will answer, "Lord, to whom shall we go? You have the words of eternal life."

13.
God's Voice
and Our Response

The Lord God has spoken;
who can but prophesy? (3:8).

Amos, that dour and taciturn son of the land, was not a man whose mind and soul could easily be read. An outsider would have a hard time discerning what struggles went on within him. Amos was completely different from Jeremiah in this respect. Jeremiah was a sensitive man whose mind and soul were an open book to those around him. He spoke candidly about his inner conflicts and let it be known how difficult it was for him to follow his prophetic calling, how he struggled against it, and how it finally burned like a fire within his bones, for the Lord was too strong for him.

Amos did not speak of such personal difficulties — but that doesn't mean he never had them. His calling as prophet was first and foremost to announce to his own people their destruction. That is not an easy assignment for someone with *love* in his heart. Loveless people have no difficulty talking about God's judgments, but Jesus wept about them.

Because all of God's prophets dearly loved their people, they found the task of preaching judgment almost too much to bear. It was not easy, then, for a simple sheep farmer and livestock dealer to preach to the cultured inhabitants of the city. To make it even more difficult, his hearers replied by saying, "You shall not prophesy."

Prophesying is not easy. Although Amos did not talk about his difficulties, we see when we read between the lines that this "burden bearer" — for that's what his name means — had a hard time of it. If Amos had been able to rid himself of this burden, he would have done so. But it was impossible. He could not stop prophesying, for he was driven by divine necessity. "The Lord God has spoken; who can but prophesy?" When God's voice is heard, the prophet *must* respond by speaking.

"The Lord God has spoken." Here Amos tells us something about God's voice and what it sounds like. He compares that voice to the roaring of a lion. In the immediately preceding parallel sentence, we read: "The lion has roared; who will but fear?"

We may find this comparison puzzling. The roaring of a lion, after all, is hardly a pleasing or comforting sound. How, then, can Amos compare God's voice to such a sound? The God who commands the children bearing His image to seek all that is lovely and beautiful must be perfect in His own beauty — and therefore His voice must be beautiful! The voices of some of His creatures are certainly very beautiful. Thus the most lovely of all human voices must be enchantingly beautiful. The lovely harmony of the voices of the angels is beyond our imagination. But the voice of God Himself, who is the Creator of all those voices, must be far more beautiful than any of them.

The Bible gives us some small idea of this when it compares the voice of God to the most lovely voice we have heard here on earth — the voice of our mother. We read that God comforts His people as a mother comforts her children (Is. 66:13). Does that voice sound like a lion's roar? Of course not!

The same voice that tells us so tenderly that He is not angry and does not intend to scold us can turn into a lion's roar when God does become angry. But in this anger, God remains holy and beautiful, for He makes all things — including His voice — beautiful *in His own time.* The same voice that can whisper so softly in the trees in the garden can rage and roar in a frightening way when it comes to the sins of His people.

God had good reason to be angry at Israel. In political and social life, the Israelites regarded self-interest, rather than the will of God, as the highest law. (Is it any different among us?) Whatever served to increase one's own power and riches was accepted as the norm, even if it violated the covenant relationship with God and involved oppressing the poor.

As far as the life of the church was concerned, the forms were maintained, but the people felt that religion was costing them too much and was at bottom harmful to society. That's what the grain dealers said as they waited impatiently for the end of the sabbath so they could again sell their provisions (8:5). During the singing in the temple, their minds were on their business; the rattling of money, such as we still hear in church today, reminded them of the marketplace!

Is it any wonder that God was angry and roared like a lion? His anger was the result not so much of a feeling that His rights had been violated but of a love that was scorned. God was angry at Damascus and Gaza because they failed to honor His holiness. But His wrath toward Israel was different and much greater. It was a wrath born of holy jealousy and scorned love.

It is much more painful when your wife or one of your best friends betrays you or does something to hurt you than when a stranger does so. Likewise, it hurts God very deeply when His chosen people, with whom He has made a covenant, betray Him. This drags God's *name* and His *covenant* through the mud. Therefore Amos deliberately uses God's covenant name in this context: the Lord God has spoken, Yahweh, the God of the covenant.

Like a wounded animal, the Lord now emerges from His dwelling place. His voice is a terrible sound to listen to. The lion has roared! The Lord has spoken! Now the loving, motherly voice of our heavenly Father is no longer tender and comforting. What we hear is the frightful roar of a wounded love. The Lord has spoken, and what a voice He has! That voice has power!

When God speaks, something happens. We can speak of the "power" of man's words only in a derived, secondary sense, for in the final analysis such power belongs to the Lord alone. When He speaks, it is accomplished.

No human being knows the complete power of God's Words or has heard the complete sound of His voice. Just as we can only form a *general* idea of the power of the storm from the wreckage washed up on the beaches and the branches torn from the trees, we sense the power of God's voice only from the *consequences.*

Israel saw those consequences. Many judgments were visited upon Israel in those days. The Israelites were afflicted with mildew and earthquake, with locusts, crop failures and wars (4:7-10). No doubt many of them sought "natural causes" for these catastrophes, but Amos explained that no evil befalls a city unless the Lord has done it (3:6). In all those judgments, the Lord God was speaking.

God no longer speaks directly from heaven to any of us as He used to speak to Abraham, Jacob, Samuel, and the prophets. Yet we are in a position to hear God's voice all the same. The Lord God has spoken in the Bible, and He has spoken in history. The Lord God speaks in your life's minor episodes and major turning points. He also speaks eloquently through the evil that befalls the city and the countryside alike.

To modern man, who wants to restrict the size of families before we wind up with too little food and too many people, the Lord says, "Don't forget about Me." And then He makes the world poorer than ever. He prevents the building of a modern tower of Babel not by confusing the languages but by bringing unemployment. The Lord God speaks in many different ways.

Ashkelon and Damascus, Paris and London, Washington and Moscow aren't even aware of His voice — to say nothing of His apparent anger. But God's children, who understand Him when He speaks, recognize the voice of the Lord that strips the leaves and branches from the trees. In His temple they honor Him.

Honoring Him does not mean blaming everything on the godless world; it means recognizing that we have aroused His anger through our own unfaithfulness. This makes us fearful. Trembling we say to each other:

The lion has roared;
who will not fear?
The Lord God has spoken;
who can but prophesy?

Amos expected two kinds of results from the Lord's Words. By asking the same type of question twice, he made it clear that he considered it a foregone conclusion that everyone would be afraid and everyone would prophesy. Yet, then as now, things didn't always go the way Amos — or anyone else, for that matter — would have preferred. The nations living around Israel went their own merry way, while in Israel the prophet had to threaten those who were "at ease in Zion."

History repeats itself. God is patient and faithful in speaking to man, but man remains unmoved. What is there to be *afraid* of, after all? There is, of course, a general fear that circumstances will get even worse, and that poverty will increase. But do we see any evidence of a genuine "fear of the Lord"? I'm afraid not. What we do not see is people *fleeing* from the God who roars like a lion or people *taking refuge* in the God who calls us like a father.

Do *we* fear the Lord? There are many who may have shivered at the thought of the wrath to come and been frightened at the prospect of death, but has such fear born fruit in the form of repentance and conversion? Or was it like a morning cloud that passed quickly?

"The lion has roared; who will not fear?"

Amos expected a second result from the sound of God's voice, for he asked, "Who can but prophesy?" God's Word has a double effect on His people. It shatters, but also heals. It creates fear, but also reassures us. It kills and revives. It renders us speechless with terror, but later loosens our tongues. The first fruit of God's voice is: Who will not fear? The second is: Who can but prophesy?

Amos, whose own soul shivered at the majesty of God and the voice of the roaring lion, then proceeded to *prophesy*. Because he wanted his people to escape judgment, and because he wished to stand up for the holiness of God's name and covenant, he could no longer remain silent. He voiced his objections to the spirit of the age. He protested loudly against Israel's degenerate way of life.

"Who can but prophesy?"

We have certainly made a great deal of progress since the days of Amos. In those days the prophet wasn't even allowed to say his piece. His lips were sealed, and he was told, "You shall not prophesy." Prophets in our time, however, are allowed to speak freely. We heap the greatest honors on the prophet who speaks most earnestly of God's judgments. We tell each other that it's time for the prophet to really lay it on the line, and then we virtually enjoy it as he tells us off. That's real progress!

Or is it the opposite of progress? I, for one, don't believe it represents progress, for to adopt such an attitude or outlook is to make two fundamental errors. First, we believe that encouraging the prophet to prophesy brings us closer to the Kingdom of heaven than *forbidding* him to prophesy. That's certainly a mistake, for an *aroused* and *angry* Saul (i.e., Paul) is closer to conversion than an indifferent Pharisee.

The second mistake we make is that we narrow down the all-embracing question "Who can but prophesy?" to the question "What preacher can but prophesy?" Prophesying and testifying, we reason, involves *office,* but in the process we forget that we all have an office, that every Christian is a prophet called to confess the name of Christ.

Is there anyone who really prophesies in our time? Is there anyone in God's prophesying church who can properly be called a prophet? Is there anyone who decries the sins of our time in word and deed? Is there anyone who points triumphantly to Jesus, the One who saves us from the claws of the lion?

The Lord God has spoken! Have you and I spoken? There is always a lot of talking going on, of course, but the voices sound impure. The uncertain sound of the trumpet hardly resembles the voice of a prophet.

Christians often talk about how God is judging the world — but where are the prophets? One Christian complains, "What a miserable time to be alive!" A second murmurs, "The government is too slow to act, and when it finally does act, it makes major errors." A third mutters as he walks out of church, "Today's sermon was nothing to get excited about, either."

We say, "These are bad times. Who can help but complain? There are many unjust laws. Who can help but protest? Many of the preachers are good for nothing. Who can help but be critical?"

Amos says, "The Lord has spoken. Who can help but prophesy?" There are many complainers and questioners and critics and faultfinders, but where are the prophets?

We are entering a frightening and perilous situation. The Lord's voice comes through loudly, persistently, and urgently. Listen to the Word of the Lord! Listen to the roar of the lion — and be afraid! Listen to the Father's supplication — and be not afraid! Flee God's wrath by running into His arms. Remember that the Lion who roars is also the Lamb who was slain to take away the sins of the world. Those who have learned to fear the roaring of the Lion will also be able to sing the song of the Lamb.

14.
Amazed Observers

Stand upon the palaces in Ashdod
and upon the palaces of Egypt,
and proclaim aloud:
"Assemble on the hills of Samaria,
look at the tumult seething among her people
and at the oppression in her midst" (3:9 NEB).

The prophet Amos now beats his heavy drum. He is not afraid to broadcast the sins of Israel. The godlessness and injustice within the walls of Samaria must be publicly denounced.

Heralds were sent right and left, to Ashdod, one of the cities of the Philistines, and Egypt. Those fleet messengers were given a very special assignment: they were to stand on the palaces of the heathen cities and proclaim their message. Israel's wickedness was literally to be preached from the rooftops.

All of this sounds somewhat strange to our Western ears, but in the ancient Near East it was not an unusual way of doing things. The flat roofs of the houses were suitable for making public proclamations. Thus, the people were accustomed to being addressed from some rooftop or other. The higher roofs of the palaces were especially good "pulpits," for someone speaking from them could be heard far away.

And that was where these heralds from Israel were to stand as they proclaimed their message. From those "pulpits" they would say their piece. What were they supposed to say? What message were they to proclaim aloud from the rooftops of the palaces? They were told to say:

> Assemble on Samaria's mountain
> and see what great disorder there is in that city,
> what oppression is found inside her (3:9 JB).

The people of Ashdod and Egypt were invited to an assembly. The message went especially to the wealthy, the people who lived in palaces. They were to gather on the hills around Samaria, in an open-air theater, as it were. Those who took a seat in this theater would then watch what went on in Samaria. There the heathen observers would see a show they didn't expect to see, a spectacle that would make them throw up their hands in sheer amazement.

Come, let us assemble on the hills of Samaria and watch.

I trust you understand that the sending of those messengers and the assembling of the Philistines and Egyptians on the hills around Samaria were *imaginary* events that took place in the mind of Amos. Yet this appeal to imaginary messengers and imaginary observers was more than a mere rhetorical device. The soul of the prophet was so stirred by

Israel's far-reaching wickedness that he felt compelled to express himself in ironic terms. We could almost call this bitter sarcasm on the part of Amos, who must have been very upset to mention such peoples as the Philistines and the Egyptians.

The prophet did not select these two heathen nations at random. He chose them deliberately, to put Israel to shame. If there was any sensitivity left in the inhabitants of Samaria, it must have hurt them that Ashdod and Egypt were called to witness the abuses and oppression within their walls.

Wasn't Egypt the nation that had once oppressed Israel? The memory of those days was still alive. Their fathers had been all but worked to death as slaves; they had been forced to make bricks under the lash of the slave driver's whip. They had been trampled upon and humiliated by those Egyptian tyrants. As a slave nation, Israel had suffered and despaired because of the exhausting forced labor. Finally it had come perilously close to extermination when the male children were drowned in the Nile like unwanted kittens. When a Jew heard the name *Egypt,* he muttered under his breath, "Cursed be Egypt! Death to those oppressors!"

Amos also mentioned Ashdod! The time of slavery in Egypt had already faded into the distant past, but the humiliation at the hands of the Philistines had not taken place so long ago. Hadn't Samson, Israel's national hero, been blinded and forced to do degrading work by the Philistines? Hadn't Ashdod put its proud foot on Israel's neck? Cursed be Ashdod!

That's how Egypt and Ashdod had treated Israel. "They have oppressed us from the very beginning," said Israel. "The plowers plowed upon my back; they made long their furrows" (Ps. 129:3).

The heathens had indeed made deep furrows in the backs of the defenseless, but later they had met their match, indeed, their master — in cruelty. Their master was Israel, the former slave!

When those who once were nothing become something, when slaves become masters, they often turn out to be the most cruel masters of all. The Communists in Russia, who are the "exploited" people of an earlier era, far exceed the old Czarist regime in cruelty. They represent a modern example of this principle. Israel is an apt example from ancient times.

Although God repeatedly reminded His people that they had once been slaves, in the hope that this awareness would make them merciful and compassionate, the nation that was supposed to mirror the virtues of God went in the opposite direction. Their years in bondage did not lead them to forswear oppression. Instead they developed an appetite for it. What slavery taught them was not mercy but cruelty. Apparently the Israelites were apt pupils and learned from their masters some refined and sophisticated techniques of tyranny. Soon they were even better at it than their teachers. They strangled weaker members of their own nation and society in a manner unparalleled in Egypt and Ashdod.

This is what Ashdod and Egypt were now invited to observe! What successful teachers they had been! What "thankful" pupils the Israelites were! Ashdod and Egypt could now learn from their former slaves. "Assemble on the hills of Samaria and watch!" The jaws of the observers would drop in amazement as they discovered that even greater cruelty is possible.

There are numerous indications that Israel was more cruel than the Egyptians and Philistines had ever thought of being. In the first place, the heathens oppressed *foreigners,* but the inhabitants of Samaria oppressed their own people, lying on garments taken in pledge and selling the needy for the price of a pair of shoes. In the second place, their excessive cruelty is apparent from the very words chosen by Amos to depict the spectacle to be observed:

> Look at the tumult seething among her people
> and at the oppression in her midst;

what do they care for honesty
who hoard in their palaces the gains of crimes and violence?
   (3:9-10 NEB).

That's what these heathens were invited to watch.

By *tumult* Amos meant a total reversal of the established order, so that white was called black and wrong right.
The Israelites had finally become so used to this that they
no longer *knew* how to do good. They had lost the most
fundamental and elementary moral concepts. In this regard
they were worse than the Egyptian Pharaoh, who at least
had an idea of his offense against the Lord — even if he did
then harden his heart.

Meanwhile, the rich in Samaria profited from the
oppression of the poor. In their palaces they hoarded their
ill-gotten gains. But they were not aware that gathering
those treasures meant filling their homes with sin and violence,
any more than they were aware that such treasures would
bring the wrath of God upon them on the day of judgment!

Yes, Ashdod and Egypt should certainly come and see
the spectacle in Samaria. They, too, knew what it was to
exploit the poor, but they still had much to learn from
Samaria, that upstart, that former slave! Therefore it will be
easier for Ashdod and Egypt on the day of judgment than
for Samaria.

The church of the Lord still has its observers today,
both visible and invisible. The visible observers are the
children of the world. We live *in* the world, and what we do
is a matter of public record. This world has long ago closed
its ears to the preaching of the Word, but it still keeps an
eye on the conduct of Christians. It is a silent tribute to the
power of the gospel that the world always expects something
more from the church — a holier life, a more sensitive conscience. Unbelievers gather around the church in large
crowds and pay careful attention to what goes on there.
They know how to point out the smallest stain on the suit
you're wearing, and they quickly become scornful if the
offenders are "pious" people who pretend to "know better."

In one way, such criticism is unfair and can be explained in large measure as the result of feelings of enmity. It is based on the false assumption that anyone who goes to church is somehow "holier." The fact of the matter is that church members are also stumbling sinners.

But in another way, this criticism is justified. The world is right in expecting more of us, for we have our roots in a special source of life and strength. We cannot escape the world's criticism simply by pointing to its "enmity." Claiming that the world's opinion does not concern us and that the world should mind its own business is false pride.

In fact, it is an example of oppression, an oppression of souls, for we are supposed to be a visible proclamation and should be winning our neighbor for Christ. If there is no difference at all between our way of life and the world's lifestyle, if we join in the swindling and deceit and recklessness and selfishness, then the world will ask itself in bewilderment why it should move from Ahsdod to Samaria and enter the Kingdom of God. Then we are blocking the sinner's way to heaven, which means we are getting in Christ's way. In our own self-righteousness, we endanger the eternal welfare of the wayward sinner. Therefore we must never forget about the observers gathered around the walls of Samaria.

In addition to the visible observers, there are also invisible observers. First of all, there are the devils, who dance a frenzied dance of joy when they see that the church is more wicked than the world. Even if the church were only the world's equal in wickedness, the sin of the church would be ten times worse than that of the world. Therefore the devils dance themselves into an ecstatic frenzy, for they know as well as you do that faith without works is dead. The devil always delights in death — especially the death of the church. Therefore we would do well to remember that the eyes of those invisible observers are upon us.

There are also observers in heaven. The letter to the Hebrews informs us that we are surrounded by a great cloud of witnesses. The inhabitants of heaven observe the life of the church as if they were seated in an amphitheater. In animated excitement they watch how the church conducts itself. There is great surprise and disappointment among God's angels whenever the church relents in its struggle, but great joy over a single sinner who repents. There are also angels assembled on the hills around Samaria.

Finally, there is someone else whose eye is always on you. He is the invisible One who observes all your deeds, listens to all your conversations, and knows all your thoughts. He is aware of all your sins and keeps track of them as no one else can. One day He will open His books and make them public, so that even Ashdod and Egypt will hear what you have done.

Church of the Lord, think of all those observers assembled on the hills around Samaria!

15.
Silent
Witnesses

As the shepherd rescues from the mouth of the lion two legs, or a piece of an ear, so shall the people of Israel who dwell in Samaria be rescued, with the corner of a couch and part of a bed (3:12).

Here Amos, the prophet of doom, declares that the children of Israel will be "rescued." At last! The prophet has some good news for us!

He certainly doesn't seem eager to promise deliverance. He's much better at blowing the trumpet to announce judgment. Now, in any event, we can relax again. The sun is breaking through the storm clouds. The frightening roar of the lion has ceased. The children of Israel will be saved!

That's what it *sounds* like — but don't raise your hopes too high. Don't forget to ask *how* the children of Israel will be saved. Is Amos talking about a joyous triumph? If only he were!

What Amos is telling us is that the children of Israel will be rescued as a shepherd rescues two legs or a piece of an ear from the lion's mouth. Suppose a lion enters a sheep-fold and kills a sheep. Later the frightened shepherd can find no trace of the poor animal except a couple of legs and a piece of an ear. Would you then say that the sheep had been *rescued?* There's virtually nothing left of the animal!

Here we must take the word *rescue* with a grain of salt. It's an example of prophetic irony. This miserable rescue is no rescue at all, for the animal has been totally destroyed!

Thus we have judgment again. The storm clouds aren't dispersing after all. The lion is still roaring.

Amos's reference to sheep and the shepherd is only an analogy. Reality, unfortunately, is even more disturbing. In a harshly realistic way, the prophet sketches the catastrophe that will befall Israel. Amos tells us that the children of Israel will be saved with the corner of a couch and part of a bed, that is, with perhaps one large cushion and some sort of bedspread or covering.

To understand this frightful picture of Israel's woe, we must assume that the horrible earthquake to which Amos referred (1:1) woke the inhabitants of Samaria from their sleep. The earth rumbled and shook, while the walls creaked and collapsed. Then, in their panic, people grabbed whatever was at hand and fled. We have also seen this sort of thing in the twentieth century, as refugees from modern warfare flee from advancing armies, carrying a few worthless objects in their hands and on their backs. One might be carrying a bird cage, and another might push a baby carriage. That's all they were able to "save."

The inhabitants of Samaria became such refugees. As the walls of their ivory palaces collapsed, they could save none of the treasures they had accumulated. They fled with nothing more than a large cushion and a bedspread on which they happened to be sleeping. While most of them died a horrible death in the frightful panic, there were a few Israelites who managed to escape with blankets, linens, or parts of their beds. Just as a shepherd comes home and has nothing more to show for his once beautiful flock than a couple of legs or a piece of an ear, so the children of Israel, who were once so rich and totally at ease in their palaces, would escape with a few blankets or part of a bed.

Thus the Israelites would indeed be rescued. But don't ask what kind of rescue awaited them!

From reality we return to the analogy of the shepherd and the sheep slain by the lion. As a sheep farmer, Amos must have suffered such losses from time to time. When he was called upon to proclaim judgment, he did not make use of analogies that would not be understood but turned to everyday occurrences to show that the "rescue" Israel could expect was really no rescue at all.

Yet there is more to this analogy. Amos, who knew the laws of the Lord as well as he knew the practical side of the life of a shepherd, was certainly alluding to one of those laws when he spoke of the shepherd who brings back some remnant of the slain sheep. In Exodus 22:10-13 we read:

> If a man delivers to his neighbor an ass or an ox or a sheep or any beast to keep, and it dies or is hurt or is driven away, without anyone seeing it, an oath by the Lord shall be between them both to see whether he has not put his hand to his neighbor's property; and the owner shall accept the oath, and he shall not make restitution. But if it is stolen from him, he shall make restitution to its owner. If it is torn by beasts, let him bring it as evidence; he shall not make restitution for what has been torn.

Thus when a shepherd gathered together what was left of a slain animal, he was not wasting his time. His own honor and personal interests were at stake. If he could not produce any remnant of the dead animal as evidence, if he could not substantiate the truth of his story by showing a leg or a piece of an ear, for example, he would be suspected of stealing the other man's property and would have to make full restitution.

This law also sheds some light on the story of Joseph and his brothers. The Mosaic laws were not yet known at that time, but there were such regulations in the laws of Hammurabi, which were then in effect. Joseph's brothers also brought back a "silent witness" in the form of Joseph's coat. It served the same purpose as a leg or a piece of an ear. It was an indication that Joseph had been killed by some animal.

These remnants were of great importance. No shepherd whose flock was attacked by a beast of prey would leave them behind. He needed them as proof. Legs and ears were his silent witnesses.

Israel's shepherd was Yahweh. Just as a shepherd is responsible for his flock, the Lord is responsible for His people, because of the covenant He has made with them. Israel's security lay in this covenant. Maintaining the covenant and preserving Israel was a matter of God's honor. If the covenant were broken and His people perished, the heathens would say, "Couldn't He protect His people?" They would laugh at the shepherd who allowed His sheep to be stolen. This the Lord could not permit.

Israel was indeed destroyed, but the *nucleus*, the remnant chosen in God's grace, was preserved. The wild branches were cut off, but the root remained. The goats were slain by wild animals, but the sheep in His pasture were protected. Israel ceased to exist as a *nation*, but the individual believers survived, becoming as numerous as the grains of sand on the seashore, which can neither be measured nor numbered (Hosea 1:10).

Those believers are the legs and ears, as it were. That's

why the Lord was so concerned about the remnant of Israel. His honor was at stake. The remnant constituted legal, compelling proof of His faithfulness toward Israel. They were His silent witnesses.

This remnant certainly shrank in the course of history. Amos reports that nothing was left of David's once glorious dynasty but a fallen house (9:11). Nothing was left of the proud tree but a stump. Nothing was left of the once large flock but a couple of legs and a piece of an ear.

But the trunk of Jesse finally gave rise to the great Son of David who said, "I am the good shepherd. The good shepherd lays down his life for the sheep" (John 10:11). In order to save what He could from the mouth of the lion, He surrendered His life.

The sword is drawn against our Shepherd. He is attacked, and the sheep are scattered. But He will protect the little ones with His powerful hand. Those little ones are the legs that have been saved, the burning brands plucked from the fire, the tax-collectors and sinners, the silent and thankful witnesses of the great love and faithfulness that never lets Israel down.

Are you one of the witnesses of God's faithfulness?

Our group is becoming so large! Our membership is growing! Our church is so full!

That's wonderful! But are all of you part of the "remnant"? Many of you have been called, but are all of you chosen? Do all of you manifest the power of godliness as well as its signs? When the great opponent, the Antichrist, is let loose in the church, will no one sitting in the pew, no "member of the covenant," be slain? When the great sifting and sorting takes place, will all the "church people" turn out to be among the remnant, and will all the "wordly" people be devoured by the beast? Or will the sorting cut right through our churches and families, taking one and leaving another when two are found in one bed or one field? When the tremendous tension sets in, will the ranks of the visible church be decimated, and will the "children of Israel" be rescued as a shepherd rescues a couple of legs and a part of an ear from the lion's mouth?

I'm just asking a few questions. Don't go to sleep or let your eyes rest until you've answered them, for they are questions about eternity.

Are you one of the witnesses of God's faithfulness?

Blessed are those who come to Jesus — even without a cushion or a bedspread — as poor, miserable refugees on this earth, where they hear of earthquakes in various places. Poor and miserable as they are, He welcomes them.

Did you have any idea that the precious name of Jesus lay hidden in the miserable remains of a slaughtered flock? Jesus is present today in the misery of your shattered existence. Do you hear Him knocking?

16.
Of Cows and Fish

Listen to this, you cows of Bashan (4:1 NEB).

Amos does not show a great deal of respect for the *women* in his audience: he speaks of the women of Samaria as "cows." Without blushing or batting an eye, he says to the dignified ladies and stately matrons, "Listen to this, you cows of Bashan." That he was referring only to the women is apparent from the fact that these "cows" have "husbands." The husbands, whom they are supposed to obey, are ordered to bring home wine so all may drink (4:1).

A little later the prophet compares these same women, whom he had called "cows," to fish. He foresees a time

> when they shall take you away with hooks,
> even the last of you with fishhooks (4:2).

Neither of these comparisons is particularly flattering to the daughters of Samaria. Neither cows nor fish show signs of great intelligence. A young woman would hardly feel complimented if she were told, "Your eyes are like the eyes of cows and codfish." The women of Samaria certainly didn't appreciate Amos's less than flattering form of address. They were extremely indignant at the crude farmer from Tekoa who had the nerve to call them, the elite and cultured women of the city, cows and fish.

But God's prophets are not in the business of calling people names. Here, too, Amos's words were intended as an expression of holy indignation; they represented a proclamation of judgment.

The point of comparison between the women of Samaria, on the one hand, and cows and fish, on the other, had nothing to do with outward appearance or intelligence. What drew the prophet's attention was not rationality but morality. Again and again he spoke out against the ethical degeneration of the people of his time; he was uncompromising in his denunciation of the moral decay and increasing lawlessness.

Things were bad enough among the men: "A man and his father go in to the same maiden, so that my holy name is profaned" (2:7). But the women weren't making things any better. Instead of restraining the unbridled passions of the men by a chaste, modest attitude, they pushed the men even further. The influence they exercised was bad, rather than good. In fact, the women were the quiet instigators of the shameless oppression of the poor; it was at their urging that the poor were sold for the price of a pair of shoes. They incited the men to violence. They became hyenas!

Never cross a woman!

What was the background of these comments by Amos? During the prosperity which Israel enjoyed under Jeroboam II, people in the cities especially got used to luxury. The women had it particularly good. That's why Amos compares them to "cows of Bashan," for the fruitful countryside of Bashan was famous for its excellent pastures and abundant

vegetation. Good-looking, fat cattle were raised there. This
was the kind of abundance in which the wives of the important men of Samaria lived. But were they content with their
luxury? Not at all. The more they got, the more they demanded. Ordinary incomes did not suffice to satisfy their
extravagant demands. But these sophisticated women knew
how to overcome such limitations. They encouraged their
husbands to turn to violence and theft: the little man would
have to pay. The important thing was for these women to
satisfy their appetites for luxury. It was especially important
to them that there be wine on the table. In the morning, as
their husbands left for the day's business, they told them to
be sure to bring home some wine to drink that evening.

The *women,* then, were the driving force behind the
scenes. The injustice and violence in Israel must in large
measure be laid at the doorstep of these women of luxury
who, like the cows of Bashan, could not do without their
rich pastures. Therefore Amos rightly held the women
responsible:

> Listen to this word, you cows of Bashan
> living in the mountain of Samaria,
> oppressing the needy, crushing the poor,
> saying to your husbands, "Bring us something to drink!" (4:1 JB).

Things couldn't go on this way forever. Sin does not
stand still. Degeneration in social life does not stop at some
point but penetrates even into the marriage relationship.
Yet, here as elsewhere, the "forms" remained intact. These
women were daughters of Sarah, just as their husbands were
children of Abraham. "We have never served anyone,"
these men maintained — "except our wives." The daughters
of Sarah gave orders to their husbands while pretending to
be subordinate.

There will come a time, Amos prophesies, when these
cows will be removed from their rich pastures, when they
will be torn from the luxurious lives they lead in their palaces

— here he switches to another analogy — just as fish are sometimes pulled suddenly and unexpectedly out of the pleasant environment in which they are at home.

> The Lord God has sworn by his holiness
> that, behold, the days are coming upon you,
> when they shall take you away with hooks,
> even the last of you* with fishhooks (4:2).

A fish stupidly surrenders its life by swallowing the tasty bait, failing to see the dangerous fishhook inside. People are like fish in this respect. Someone who wanders far and wide in search of luxury will perish before long and be cursed. That's something you can count on. This truth also applied to the women of Samaria. Their love of luxury and abundance would lead to their downfall. Their abundance would become total poverty. Turning again to the somber things to come, Amos prophesied that Samaria would be beseiged. The walls would be so completely battered down that there would be a hole in the wall for each woman, and through it she would be taken out of the city. No detour would be necessary: "Out you will go, each by the nearest breach in the wall" (4:3 JB).

Instead of leading a life of luxury in the palace, these women would wind up in exile in a land where they would be outcasts — perhaps in faraway Armenia. Amos warned them: "You shall be cast forth into Harmon" (4:3).†

The influence a woman can exercise — whether for good or ill — can hardly be overestimated. A woman can act the part of an angel or of a devil. She can be a preserving or a corrupting influence. She can be a Monica (the mother of Augustine) or a Jezebel (the wife of Ahab). Whatever role she chooses, she is usually consistent.

---

*What Amos means here, of course, is a deportation to the last man — or better, the last woman.

†My guess is that *Harmon* stands for Armenia. This is a difficult passage, and it is translated rather freely in older versions of the Bible. It is also possible that *Harmon* means some other country.

It is no exaggeration to say that world history, the history of the church, and the course of many a man's life has been dominated and determined by women. The deeds of many of the men who may or may not have played a role in history can be explained in terms of the women in their lives. In the background of many a conflict or murder lurks a woman. Therefore it is extremely important for a young man to choose the right woman as his wife. So much depends on it. Even his salvation may be at stake.

Blessed the man who chooses a God-fearing wife. She will have a strong and salutary influence on him. Woe to the man who is more interested in wealth and physical beauty, who gives the "cows of Bashan" an appreciative look.

The devil was certainly well aware of woman's potential influence for evil. The drama of Samaria, where the women led their husbands down the wrong path, is really only a sequel to what happened in Paradise. The devil probably knew that he personally would have no influence on Adam. A frontal assault was bound to fail. Therefore he decided to attack Adam in a more subtle way. He let the woman represent him. He approached Adam indirectly, appealing to him through his lovely wife Eve. It is much more dangerous when a woman entices a man down the path of sin than when the devil himself does it. The method used by the devil in Paradise has been in regular use ever since.

He still uses it successfully today — in our society and marriage relationships. The conditions in Samaria are not that far removed from our lives, although there are doubtless some differences. The women of Samaria wanted to preserve their lives of luxury at all costs and maintain their "position" in society. To achieve this goal, they encouraged their husbands to oppress the poor and even use violence against them.

Modern woman also wants to preserve her life of luxury. A large family would quickly put an end to this dream. The steps modern women take to make sure they will "enjoy life as much as possible" are a bit different. The poor are no longer strangled. Instead, these women smother their own children in the womb.

We have become somewhat more civilized since the days of Samaria. We favor philanthropy and give to the poor — but we murder the unborn. That's progress!

Today we look at each other in surprise and dismay because of the crisis! Many breaches have been opened in the walls of our national prosperity and our personal lives. Each of us must pass through them into bitter exile in the land of poverty, the unknown and feared "Harmon." We just can't reconcile ourselves to the idea.

We see sadness in the vacant eyes of the "cows of Bashan" torn from their rich pastures and the staring eyes of the fish yanked abruptly out of their element. But what is there to be sad about? Have we forgotten so quickly that the prosperous years in the recent past were a time of dishonesty and wasteful luxury, a time when the sins of the "church" cried out to heaven? Can we think back calmly to that time without turning red with shame? Is it really so strange that God *always* stands by His Word? Does it surprise you that Bashan's cows are *always* driven into barren pastures, and that unwary fish are *always* pulled out of the water?

Maybe our surprise will lead us to take firm control of ourselves. Maybe the unknown land of Harmon will turn out to be a pasture full of spiritual nourishment. Maybe the era of poverty will be a period of overflowing grace.

Listen to this, you cows and fish!

17. Clean Teeth

And that is why I left your teeth clean in all
your towns,
left you without bread in all your villages;
and yet you never came back to me (4:6 JB).

"I left your *teeth clean,*" the Lord declares. This expression is immediately explained: "I left you without bread." In this case, then, clean teeth are a sign of famine. Those "clean teeth" were not a blessing but a *curse.* The famine was so complete that no one got a bite to eat — and therefore no one's teeth were in danger of decaying. So great was the hunger that the last particles of food stuck between the teeth had been extracted and eaten long ago.

Here Amos was again using irony. We could almost call it sarcasm. Israel celebrated its joyful festivals of sacrifice and held sacrificial meals, all to the greater glory of Yahweh. The Israelites thought that these celebrations would please God.

Now Amos gave them God's response. As a way of thanking them for their offerings, God took the last crumbs of bread away. That's how disgusted He was. He repaid them with clean teeth!*

Thus the crisis was no trifling matter. It represented a fearful plunge from the level of prosperity that had been attained. The people became paupers and lived in famine and misery.

Furthermore, this crisis was not limited to a few segments of the population. It was restricted neither to the cities nor to the countryside. The prophet says explicitly that the misery penetrated to "all your towns" and "all your villages." Thus, even the smallest settlements were affected.

Today we would call such a crisis a *structural* crisis. At issue was the structure of the time. Everywhere one saw the same spectacle — in every business, in towns, in villages, and among the workers and farmers. The crisis and malaise affected "all your towns and villages."

This state of affairs did not come about *unexpectedly,* as the rest of the fourth chapter of Amos makes clear. When we realize this, the Lord's somber refrain "Yet you never came back to me" sounds even more somber.

The rain had already stopped three months before the harvest. That in itself was fatal for a harvest in Palestine; it heralded the approach of famine. Furthermore, Amos 4 also mentions pestilence and catastrophes resulting from war (4:10), as Israel is reminded how it had been saved in the nick of time when God overthrew Sodom and Gomorrah, just as a burning brand is plucked from the fire (4:11). Thus

---

*Some interpreters, thinking of the prosperity in Amos's time, take this verse to mean: even *if* I were to leave you with clean teeth, you still would not repent. There is no compelling reason for such a departure from the text. We do not know everything about Jeroboam's long reign. Catastrophes such as the ones described here could well have taken place during his reign, even if they are not mentioned in the historical books of the Bible. They may even have taken place before Jeroboam's time.

the specter of hunger approached gradually. First came war, then pestilence, then crop failure and drought, all of which finally led to complete poverty in all the towns and villages.

It almost seems that Amos was here describing *our* time with its needs and problems. Doesn't his description correspond to what has happened recently? First came the mighty upheavel of two world wars. Later — partly as a result of these upheavals — came poverty and clean teeth in many areas. There was no lack ot warnıng of the coming judgment. Today's crisis certainly did not come about unexpectedly. "Yet you never came back to me," the Lord complains.

As we examine these things from God's point of view, we must take a sober look at the facts themselves. The facts remind us of famine and clean teeth! And what is God's standpoint? He says, "*I* am the One who gave you cleanness of teeth and lack of bread."

This revelation also affects our own point of view. What God says here is not the kind of thing we normally say to one another, nor is it the kind of thing we read in newspapers. *I* am the One! Some people regard it as old-fashioned to speak of God's judgments in such a context. Others explain the problems of our time on the basis of earthly factors, such as economic conditions, international tensions, and mistakes made by the government. And there is indeed a place for this kind of explanation — provided we do not forget that God is at work in and behind all of this. *I* am the One!

Amos points to such ordinary earthly phenomena as rain, drought, shortages, and crumbs of bread — and then ascribes everything to *God's* control. *I* am the One who sends famine! *I,* the Lord, am the One who sends rain and withholds rain.

We should also look at our *spiritual* problems in this light. Our economic problems are serious, very serious, but even more serious is the great spiritual problem of our time, namely, that we disregard God and no longer think of Him. We read and reread the book of our economic woes, but we forget that God Himself is the Author of the book of our life. This is a grave spiritual problem that we should not take lightly.

When we have more than enough bread, we do not see the divine *Giver,* and when we are short of bread, we forget who is withholding it. Everything revolves around ourselves, and we give no thought whatsoever to God. In *theory,* of course, we do consider God. In theory, everything always falls into place. But what do we do in *practice* when ships sail into our harbor, some of them filled with blessings from God and others with His judgments?

If we are aware that no evil befalls a city unless the Lord has done it, we are led to ask the great question: Why? This question is not unknown to us. On the contrary, it rises in our minds regularly. Usually we resist the impulse to ask this question, for we regard it as a sign of resentment, believing that it betrays doubt about God's providence and guidance.

Often there is no need to ask why. When our "Why?" is answered with a "Because," is the misfortune that we now understand any easier to bear than the suffering we do not understand? In many cases, the burden will seem even heavier when it has been understood.

Yet we may and should ask why, even if God answers us with His "Because." That's the answer He gives in the fourth chapter of Amos.* He points to the cause of our economic problems and physical suffering, for He wants us to know what the source of our misery is. The causes are *not* to be found where we would ordinarily look for them: they are spiritual, not natural.

God's "Because" will surprise and frighten us. Let's listen!

---

*The word *because* is not present in the original text, but it does come out clearly in the contrast drawn there. The sending of the famine is presented as a sign of God's displeasure at the religious practices freely adopted by Israel. Thus the sequence is one of cause and effect.

18.
The Great
"Because"

*And that is why I left your teeth clean in all
your towns,
left you without bread in all your villages;
and yet you never came back to me (4:6 JB).*

When God's judgment strikes on earth, it doesn't take
us long to come up with the *causes.* We let spiritual motives
play a role in our investigation. We point to the frightful
disregard of God, the abominable transgression of His commandments, and the foolishness of civilized modern man
who believes that God no longer plays a part in directing the
affairs of this world. We say, "Things were bound to go
wrong! God had to intervene." We believe we have correctly
diagnosed the cause of the crisis: it is the *influence of godlessness.*

In doing this, we make the same spiritual mistake Israel
made. When there was talk of God's judgments, the Israelites

always looked *elsewhere* — to the godless heathens. Never did they look at themselves. Therefore those pious Israelites were in for a great shock. The prophet corrected them by teaching them to look first at *their own sins.*

Amos pointed to the cause of the catastrophes, and it was not all the godlessness. Rather, the object of God's displeasure was all the "piety." In God's eyes, false piety is as disgusting as godlessness. Remember that, Israel.

"Because of this, I left you with clean teeth." Because of what? The answer is to be sought in the two preceding verses:

> Go to Bethel, and sin,
> to Gilgal, and sin your hardest!
> Offer your sacrifices each morning
> and your tithes on the third day,
> burn leavened dough as a sacrifice with praise,
> announce your voluntary offerings, make them public,
> for this is what makes you happy, sons of Israel (4:4-5 JB).

Here Amos uses irony again. What he means by this invitation to go to Bethel is: "Keep it up with your pious practices! Bring your sacrifices and tithes faithfully, and especially your freewill offerings! Do you think you'll please God that way? I tell you He'll be displeased instead. Despite your piety — in fact, because of it — He's showing signs of displeasure."

Now you can be sure that Israel understood not a word that Amos was saying. No doubt the Israelites thought to themselves, "Prophets are always looking for something to complain about. If you don't sacrifice, they're unhappy. If you do sacrifice, often and voluntarily, as we do, they're still unhappy. You just can't win."

Those Israelites believed they were doing just what God expected of them. Many bands of pilgrims traveled from one end of the holy land to the other during the time of Amos. Apparently they even went outside Israel's borders to Beersheba and sacrificed to the Lord there (5:5). With great care and precision, they chose holy places to sacrifice. Wasn't *Bethel* the place where the Lord appeared to Jacob, the place where the altar had stood? And had the Lord not said to Jacob, "Arise, go up to Bethel, and make an altar"? (Gen. 35:1). And wasn't *Gilgal* the place where the covenant with the Lord was renewed under Joshua? Then how could Amos say, "Go to Bethel, and sin"? How could a journey to such a holy place be sinful? Was there no holy tradition at Bethel? Furthermore, wasn't it wonderful that sacrifices were being brought? Freewill offerings were being made! The Israelites simply could not understand what Amos was driving at.

He could hardly object to the offering of sacrifices, and yet he did. He objected not to the sacrifices as such, but to *how* and *where* they were made.

He objected first to the site chosen! People went to Bethel, Gilgal and Beersheba to serve God. The services in those places were conducted in a very dignified and edifying way. Perhaps the worshipers even exchanged impressions of how cold and formal the services of the "official church" in Jerusalem were. But holding services in places like Bethel meant going *outside the church* (i.e., Jerusalem). Jerusalem — and nowhere else — was the holy place where the Lord wanted to be served. To offer sacrifices elsewhere and to worship God elsewhere — however dignified the services might be — was to engage in a religion of *man's own devising*. Even if the service was conducted in the name of Yahweh, it was simply a sin against the second commandment, the commandment that forbids us to "worship him in any other way than he has commanded in his Word" *(Heidelberg Catechism,* Answer 96). God Himself had stipulated in His law:

> You shall demolish all the sanctuaries where the nations whose place you are taking worship their gods, on mountain-tops and hills and under every spreading tree. You shall pull down their altars and break their sacred pillars, burn their sacred poles and hack down the idols of their gods and thus blot out the name of them from that place.
>
> You shall not follow such practices in the worship of the Lord your God, but you shall resort to the place which the Lord your

God will choose out of all your tribes to receive his Name that it
may dwell there. There you shall come and bring your whole-
offerings and sacrifices, your tithes and contributions, your vows
and freewill offerings, and the first-born of your herds and flocks
(Deut. 12:2-6 NEB).

Because of this law, sacrificing at Bethel and Gilgal was a
sin. Therefore Amos later testified that seeking Bethel meant
not seeking the Lord: "Seek me and live; but do not seek
Bethel" (5:4-5). It was the first Jeroboam who had led Israel
into sin by means of this man-made religion.*

Amos's second objection was against the *how,* that is,
against the beliefs of those who brought the sacrifices. Even
if they would henceforth offer their sacrifices in Jerusalem,
God's displeasure still would not vanish entirely, for their
beliefs were in need of change. One could perhaps overlook
the use of "leavened" bread in their offerings — which was
unlawful — and even forgive their eagerness to draw attention
to their offerings. (It appeared that they were more interested
in being well-known among men than in giving thanks to
God.) But the worst thing was the great gap between their
religious fervor and their way of life, between the testimony
of their words and the testimony of their deeds. They lay
down beside the altars on garments taken in pledge and
drank the wine of those who had been fined, and while they
did so, they sang their psalms so loudly that the moans of
the poor and the miserable were drowned out. They made a
great point of being pious, but under cover of darkness they
went about their wickedness. Father and son would meet —

---

*There is some disagreement among scholars as to whether Amos
was objecting against the unlawful cultic practices which these Israelites
devised for themselves or against their mistaken attitudes and almost
heathen outlook. It seems to me that he was objecting against *both.* Amos
was well aware that *Zion* is God's dwelling place (1:2). Offering sacrifices
on a mountain was permitted only if there was no central holy place. After
Israel was divided into the two kingdoms, the inhabitants of the kingdom
of the ten tribes had a strong — but still insufficient — excuse for not
coming to *Jerusalem.*

to the surprise and shame of both — in the bedroom of some young woman whom both hoped to seduce.

Thus Amos saw social injustice, large-scale corruption, and widespread moral decay. But still these people brought their offerings, sang their songs, and practiced their religion.

On the one hand, their worship was a religion of their own making, a religion outside the church. On the other hand, it had become a great show, a comedy. Thus the two evils exposed by Amos as the "spiritual" causes of the economic crisis are: (1) "Go to Bethel, and sin," and (2) "Announce your voluntary offerings, make them public."

"Because of this, Israel, I left you with clean teeth in all your towns and villages."

Thus the Bible gives us some reliable insight into the "causes of the crisis." The lesson applies to our own time as well as to Amos's days. Didn't the wickedness of the world call forth God's judgment from heaven? It certainly did! But that's not what concerns us at the moment. We're concerned instead with what the Lord has against *us*, against the "pious" people inside and outside the church. If there is any similarity between the crisis described by Amos and the crisis which we now face, we must seek it in what the prophet points to as the *cause* of the crisis.

The cause is obvious. The God of our time is also the God of Amos's day, and it would be strange if the two major sins of the "religious" (and smaller) half of the world were to leave Him unmoved now. These two sins are altering our religion to suit ourselves and practicing our religion only in a formal, superficial way.

We love to make up our own religion. The tendency to seek a religion outside and above the church is assuming many new forms. Many people are ready to tear down the church walls, arguing that they are of no further use. The air inside those walls is much too stuffy, and there isn't enough room inside, anyway. There's no warmth and love in the church. Furthermore, what difference does the church make?

On judgment day we will be asked not to what church we belonged but whether we loved Jesus.

The fool who utters these sentiments *usurps* the judgment seat of Christ and takes it upon himself to decide "what we will be asked." This fool goes overboard with the "love of Christ" and denies Him His claim to "obedience," thereby committing a sin worse than revolution. This fool tries to kick down the church doors that Christ Himself promised to defend against the gates of hell. This fool despises the church that Christ Himself loved and founded and bought with His blood. Do you suppose the King of kings sitting at God's right hand will remain unmoved by this mutiny in the name of piety and freedom? I can assure you He won't.

That is one cause of the problems of our time. But do we recognize it as such? It is *one* cause — not the only one.

As we saw, Amos also had a second objection, namely, the gap between doctrine and conduct, a gap that represents a flaw in the outlook of those who offer their sacrifices so eagerly.

Those who choose to seek their salvation *outside* the church sometimes accuse those remaining *within* the church of Phariseeism and merely superficial piety. In general, this accusation against "the" church is unfounded. But that is no reason for us to dismiss this charge highhandedly. On the contrary, we would do well to ask ourselves whether there could be any truth to it. It is even more important that we listen to God's Word when it tells us, "Thou art the man." When God's Word talks about the person at the altar whose singing drowns out the moans of the poor and the groans of sinners, it points to you and me and says, "Thou art the man."

Isn't there too much show in our lives? Do our hearts burn with a love implanted by the Holy Spirit? Aren't our lives often one long contradiction of our confession? Isn't it true that we who call ourselves Reformed are still in need of reformation?

Israel had lost its perspective on what is primary and what is secondary. It regarded appearance as more valuable than reality and sacrifice as more valuable than what lives in the heart. When someone loses sight of norms and values so completely, he perishes like the French soldier in battle who refused to obey the order to lie down because his knapsack contained a bottle of wine without a cork: as a result, this soldier was killed by an enemy bullet. Thus, many lose their bearings and finally their lives in the great war of all ages between Christ and satan.

Who can say how many have already died spiritually because they preferred to keep up appearances (the bottle of wine in the knapsack), and how many have allowed their souls to perish because they regarded clothes, a home, and a comfortable salary as primary, despite the Biblical teaching that such things are secondary, that they are given to us if we first seek God's Kingdom?

Such are the causes of the crisis. You may cry out, "O Lord, I didn't know that my church life, my sacrifices, my prayer, and my piety were so offensive in Your eyes. Or rather, I did know it, for I have often confessed that all our righteousness is nothing more than a filthy garment to be cast aside. But now I thank You for showing me the godlessness of my piety and the wickedness of my desire to have everything my own way."

"O Lord, please accept our good works and our prayers, and be patient with the offerings we bring!"

19.
A Somber Refrain

"Yet you did not return to me," says the Lord (4:6).

All through this chapter we hear the same somber refrain: " 'Yet you did not return to me,' says the Lord." These words reveal to us the purpose the Lord had and still has in all this economic woe and physical suffering. That purpose was repentance and conversion.

In this complaint we hear God appealing to His people: "Return to Me, for why should you die, O house of Israel?" All the catastrophes were a series of appeals from heaven, coming from a God who seeks man.

Here's something for the heavens to marvel at. God

seeks man. He pleads with man, who runs away from Him and lets Him down so often. God does not ask for your sacrifices or your money, but for your heart.

In this quest, God is not passive but active, using many and various means to bring us to repentance. One of these means is giving us *too much.* "Do you not know," Paul asks, "that God's *kindness* is meant to lead you to repentance?" (Rom. 2:4). God's generosity is not without purpose. Its goal is our *conversion.*

Another means God uses is giving us *too little.* This helps us understand the famine in Amos's time. When God says, "Yet you did not return to me," it suddenly becomes clear that the clean teeth were meant not as a plague but as an expression of God's love. Being in need teaches us something: it teaches us to seek heaven, where there is abundance and glory. That is God's purpose.

But has He achieved His purpose with us? We were quite content when He gave us more than we needed. We did all sorts of things with our abundance. We delighted in this abundance, for which God had such an important purpose. But there's one thing we did not do: repent. Yet repentance was God's purpose all along.

We did take a couple of steps in that direction, but, like a motorist on a winding country road, we never arrived at the landmark seen at a distance. This is evident from the little word *to:* you never returned *to* me. The Lord's complaint is not that Israel didn't set out on the journey but that it never reached the goal.

It shouldn't surprise us that conversion is often postponed, for conversion is a terrible thing. First of all, it means admitting we're wrong, and who likes doing that? It's like getting settled in a comfortable seat in the train and then realizing that your train is going in the wrong direction. Immediately you have to get off the train, even if it's the middle of the night.

Conversion is appearing before God's judgment throne. It means hating what you loved and loving what you hated.

It means allowing your own kingdom to collapse, letting your old nature die, and attending your own funeral. It means the painful operation of plucking out your eye and cutting off the hand that leads you into sin. It means dying with Christ and being raised with Him, in order to follow Him in new obedience. That's what conversion is all about.

If we could just get it over and done with, it wouldn't be so bad, but we need to be converted *daily*. No one really *is* converted, for conversion is a continual — and painful — *process*. Conversion is not a *state* we attain but a goal we *work toward*. Being a Christian, Martin Luther pointed out, means starting all over at the beginning of each day. This is the psychological reason for the sorrowful refrain, " 'Yet you did not return to me,' says the Lord."

The Christians of our time have become too touchy about the demand that we follow the painful path of conversion every day. In an earlier era, people were burned at the stake for distributing Bibles secretly, but this sort of thing is now out of style. Unfortunately, love for the Bible has gone out of style with it. The martyrs of long ago were willing to give up their lives for the Bible, but it makes us yawn. We look at each other as if to say, "Will there ever be an end to this sermon?"

Thus we try to get around the conversion demand in all sorts of ways. Sometimes we pretend we still have plenty of time. We should remember what Bismarck once said about life's duration. It's like going to the dentist, he explained. You think the most important part is still to come, and then it's over. Jesus said in deadly earnest, "You fool, this very night you must surrender your life; you have made your money — who will get it now?" (Luke 12:20 NEB).

The Lord wants us to repent and turn to Him. When we turn away from our sins, the heavens break into song, and our lives become a song as well. The life of conversion permeates all our relationships and lets others see the splendor of God's glory. The exquisite aroma of conversion should be present in the kitchen and in the factory, in the life of the chauffeur, the travel agent, the seamstress, the office girl, the business executive, the teacher, the student, and the professor. This aroma pleases God and glorifies His name through our lives.

Then we are able to *give* something to others, even if we sacrifice ourselves in the process. Does the flower complain when its leaves wither or when the bees have taken its honey? It has bloomed! That is its glory!

20.
God and Culture

Therefore thus will I do to you, O Israel;
because I will do this to you,
prepare to meet your God, O Israel!
For lo, he who forms the mountains, and creates
*   the wind,*
and declares to man what is his thought;
who makes the morning darkness,
and treads on the heights of the earth —
the Lord, the God of hosts, is his name! (4:12-13).

Amos isn't finished yet. Although Israel has already been smashed and mangled, there are even more severe judgments coming. All the preceding plagues, i.e., famine, drought, crop failure, pestilence and war (4:6-11), will seem mere child's play in comparison to what is to come.

What is this awful judgment yet to come?

> Therefore, Israel, this is what I will do to you;
> and, because this is what I will do to you . . . (4:12 NEB).

O God, stop it! We already know what You're talking about! It's too horrible to contemplate!

Won't that somber and monotonous prophet from Tekoa ever stop preaching judgment? Hasn't he said enough already?

Because the Lord is long-suffering, He decided to answer this question. He answered a people that would not answer Him. God answered their "Why?" with a "Because," saying, "Therefore this is what I will do to you." The *therefore* goes back to the "somber refrain" repeated so often: " 'Yet you did not return to me,' says the Lord."

The call to conversion had been sounded clearly enough. First had come famine, and then drought. Mildew had caused the crops to fail, and disease had claimed many victims. Then there was war! Because of all these plagues, the country was ruined so completely that people were reminded of God's overthrow of Sodom and Gomorrah:

> I brought destruction amongst you
> as God destroyed Sodom and Gomorrah;
> you were like a brand snatched from the fire (4:11 NEB).

That was how God "cleaned house" in Palestine. He had to do it, for Israel behaved like Sodom. The conduct of the women was particularly appalling (4:1). When women become leaders in wickedness, the evil has advanced a long way. Those who act like Sodom will be treated like Sodom.

But God did not send all those plagues just to torment Israel. The five grim messengers came with an invitation: "Repent and turn to the Lord." In the garment of punishment was hidden the highest eternal good. " 'Yet you did not return to me,' says the Lord."

They let God talk to the four walls and went their own

way. They continued to resist and defy God in heaven. They thought to themselves, "God's judgments are a joke," and sometimes they even said it aloud. When their land was destroyed and lay in ruins reminiscent of Sodom, they still continued their carousing and drinking. They refused to put an end to their perversion of justice and their hypocrisy.

That was the last straw! Fiery sparks leaped from God's eyes. Now came the last threat, which actually included the final judgment of total destruction:

> Therefore, Israel, this is what I will do to you;
> and, because this is what I will do to you,
> Israel, prepare to meet your God.

These words contain a *challenge,* although the light of grace is not entirely absent from them. The curt warning to prepare to meet God is certainly frightening. Therefore this text is *not* suitable for a service of preparation for communion. Here God was calling Israel not to join in a feast of reconciliation but to do battle.* Just as a fighter in an army in ancient times might challenge a fighter of the opposing army to a duel, so the Lord was here inviting the children of Jacob to wrestle with Him, just as He had once wrestled with their father.

All God's previous warnings had fallen on deaf ears and had not led to repentance. Israel believed it was safe and secure in its own strength.

Well then, Israel, if you don't want to listen to reason, I'll knock some sense into you. Let's fight it out. Let's see who's the stronger. Step right this way! Get ready! Prepare yourself for the decisive blow, for this is what I will do to you. If you don't want peace, then we'll fight! Prepare yourself, O Israel, to meet your God!

---

*That this was the purpose is clear from the fact that in the rest of the text, God reveals Himself to Israel not as a God of grace but as a God of power and majesty.

When David accepted Goliath's challenge to do battle, the odds were by no means even. David was a simple shepherd boy armed with a slingshot, while Goliath was six cubits and a span in height. We read that the shaft of his spear was like a weaver's beam, and that his spear's head weighed 600 shekels of iron. Yet Goliath was an insignificant creature and lost the fight. His proud words turned out to be empty, hollow boasts.

But listen now to how the divine fighter makes Himself known to Israel. Take a look at His awesome dimensions and His stupendous weapons. His words are no idle boasts. He speaks the frightening truth when He says to His opponent:

> For lo, he who forms the mountains, and creates the wind,
> and declares to man what is his thought;
> who makes the morning darkness,
> and treads on the heights of the earth —
> the Lord, the God of hosts, is his name!

There is divine irony and holy humor in this expression of God's majesty and creative power. You don't want to repent, Israel? Do you want to fight with Me, then? Do you, O mighty but insignificant man of culture, wish to do battle with God? Well then, here He is! He's the One who formed the mountains and created the wind. He's the One who turns morning into darkness. He's the One who treads on the heights of the earth. Do you suppose the God of nature and the man of culture would be an even match in a fight?

The ancient world had already reached surprising cultural heights. Thus, marvels of technology and culture were not unknown in Israel during the time of Amos. The prophet speaks of artistic treasures and of couches and walls covered with ivory. There were also the "palaces" of Samaria and Jerusalem, the summer and winter homes that ranked as architectural marvels. The armies possessed up-to-date weapons.

Since the time of Amos, culture has made some awesome advances. Technology has ascended to dizzying heights. New inventions are made all the time. We live in an amazing civilization. It's almost like living in a fairy-tale world. Great is man! It may be that we have lost the ability to speak to one another "from the heart," but we are able to communicate when separated by great distances — even without telephone wires connecting us. Pilots have not yet become angels, but they certainly can fly. They don't fly all the way to heaven, but they do fly high and far. Great is man!

Now this uncultured farmer from Tekoa comes to the cultured ladies and gentlemen of Samaria, Paris, New York, and London with a simple message. He does not come to reason with them, nor does he heap scorn on their culture, for culture is also a gift of God, which He will one day sanctify for the new earth. He simply comes to tell them how great God is and how dangerous it is to be at odds with Him.

It is God who *forms the mountains.* Through the wonders of technology, man has learned to tunnel right through the mountains, so that trains can pass through them. Some trains even go over them.

But who is greater, Amos asks — the one who tunnels through mountains or the One who *makes* them? What will you do when God knocks over your tunnels and railways and houses like so many bowling pins, when that great fire destroys in one moment what you have built up over so many years? In your panic you'll call upon the mountains to cover you. And if the One who formed the mountains is not the Father to whom you are reconciled, what will you do then? Will your culture be of any help to you then, O man?

It is God who *creates the wind.* We can *make use* of the wind to propel our ships. We even use the air to broadcast beautiful music. Great is man!

But who is greater, Amos asks — the one who *uses* the wind or the One who *creates* it? And when God releases the four winds of the earth on His day of judgment, and those winds blow away all the broadcast facilities, what will you do then if the wind of the Spirit has not renewed your soul? Will your culture be of any help to you then, O man?

It is God who declares to man *what he is thinking.* Man knows a great deal and is gradually unlocking nature's secrets. There is hardly a corner anywhere that is entirely hidden from him. Great is man!

But who is greater, Amos asks — the one who knows a great deal or the One who knows everything and tells man what he is thinking? Who is greater — the One who has thought everything out or the one who can do no more than follow what has been thought by God, and only a small part of it at that? When the books are opened on that great and celebrated day and your most secret thoughts are exposed to the light of His countenance, what will you do if your name is not written in the book of life? Will your culture be of any help to you then, O man?

It is God who *makes the morning darkness.* Man is able to turn night into day. He can turn on electric lights to illumine his homes and buildings. He does wonders with gas and electricity. Great is man!

But is man powerful enough to turn morning into darkness or day into night, as God did when He made darkness descend on the Egyptians? When the sun becomes dark and the moon turns into blood on that great day, will all your palaces of light be of any help to you, O man, if the light of God's grace has not broken through to your dark soul?

One of the prophetic images in the Bible pictures the Lord using the clouds as the chariot on which He rides to judgment (see Is. 19:1). Amos also uses this image — with a small alteration — when he concludes his appeal to prepare to meet the Lord with the words:

He treads on the heights of the earth —
the Lord, the God of hosts, is his name!

This time God does not approach riding His chariot of clouds. Instead He *walks* on the clouds as on a carpet. In the storm clouds gathering above the mountain tops, Amos's prophetic ear hears the majestic footsteps of Yahweh. He is the God of Hosts, for He has a host of angels behind Him. Behold, He is coming with thousands of His angels. He is coming! He is already striding along the heights of the earth. We hear His footsteps in all the tumult and rumors of war.

Are you ready to meet Him? Would you like to do battle with Him?

I remarked earlier that the light of grace is present even in this frightening challenge. The element of grace is that God is still willing to speak to Israel (and to us). Earlier Amos had compared Israel to Sodom and Gomorrah, but God never spoke to Sodom. He destroyed Sodom and Gomorrah without a word. He is still willing to address Israel, fortunately. However gloomy and threatening His Words may be, in and behind them we hear the lament, "Why should you die, O house of Israel?"

Before the final encounter, when He returns upon the clouds of heaven, He wishes to meet us in Christ. The New Testament commentary on this Old Testament challenge is: "Behold, I stand at the door and knock; if any one hears my voice and opens the door, I will come in to him and eat with him, and he with me" (Rev. 3:20). This gives us the promise of a blessed encounter!

21.
The Living Dead

Hear this word which I take up over you in lamentation, O house of Israel (5:1).

What if you could hear the singing at your own funeral? What if you could look into your own coffin? If you could read your own obituary, you would probably be surprised at how many good things people found to say about you. Suppose you could read an announcement of your own death reporting that you died sure of your faith. (We live in doubt but die in certainty; we are disturbed in life but at peace in death.) Suppose you could watch your family mourning your death. Suppose you could observe your funeral procession moving down the street. Wouldn't that feel strange? Just thinking about it already makes us feel uneasy.

No doubt the people of Samaria also felt uneasy when Amos appeared in the city one day with torn clothes and ashes on his head, saying, "Hear this word which I take up over you in lamentation, O house of Israel." The prophet was mourning. He was reciting Israel's *obituary*.

Just as David sang his song of praise about the heroes who had fallen on Gilboa's heights, just as women sob as they trail along behind a funeral procession, so Amos was looking in spirit into Israel's coffin. The song of this sad singer was about the death of the men and women and children of Samaria. He let them hear their obituary while they were still alive. While they danced, they could watch their funeral procession pass by!

"How awful!" screamed the women of Samaria. "Why doesn't he stop with his lamentations and woe? He'll spoil our fun with his monotonous droning about death!" Some of them simply declared that Amos was insane. Given the mentality of the women of Samaria, this should not surprise us.

Was Amos in his right mind to be talking that way? Just listen to what this minstrel of death sings. What does he say in his obituary?

> Fallen, no more to rise,
> is the virgin Israel;
> forsaken on her land,
> with none to raise her up (5:2).

When Amos reads the obituary of the "virgin Israel," who has fallen and will not rise again, we are not to think of some fallen *woman*. In the poetry of the ancient Near East, it was common to personify nations. In our own language we often use pronouns like *she* and *her* to refer to nations. This virgin Israel is the nation Israel. Perhaps the word *virgin* is also intended to convey the idea of an early death. If this nation did indeed die just as the bud was blossoming, it would be all the more tragic. In any event, it is clear that the nation referred to died through some outrage, which is why

Amos speaks of her as "fallen." She lies prostrate on her own land, which drinks her blood, just as the nation had earlier drunk wine from the land. She cannot *arise*. No one can pick her up. Her face is the ashen color of death.

O beautiful, vital virgin! How the cold ground swallows your warm blood! O heroes of Israel, how you have fallen!

This is the obituary of the kingdom of the ten tribes read by the prophet.* He weeps at Israel's destruction. He kneels beside the corpse of the "virgin Israel" and sings his sorrowful dirge. The dull echo of this lament is heard against the palace walls of Samaria.

But the question again arises whether Amos was in his right mind to be talking that way. Weren't the people of Samaria right to some extent when they said that Amos was mad to be reading the obituary of the *living?*

The living? That's right! He read the obituary of the living! At the very moment when Amos was reading this obituary aloud, the "virgin Israel" was not only alive but flourishing. At the very moment when the prophet declared she was fallen, she seemed to be in the best of health. Never — not even during the famous days of Solomon — had Israel enjoyed such prosperity as under Jeroboam II, in the days of Amos. There was peace. Business was booming. People were getting rich. Israel's traditional enemies had been defeated. The danger of war seemed more remote than ever.

How could anyone maintain that the virgin Israel was fallen when she seemed stronger than ever before? How

---

*That Amos meant the kingdom of the ten tribes and was not talking about the kingdom of Judah is apparent first of all from his use of the phrase *the house of Joseph* in 5:6 and secondly from the fact that only the kingdom of the ten tribes was actually destroyed *as a nation* without rising again. There were, of course, individuals who returned from exile, i.e., the holy remnant. We read, for example, that Anna was from the tribe of Asher (Luke 2:36).

could Amos say that she lay drenched in her own blood when she was in fact drinking wine? A greater misreading of the situation is hardly conceivable. Prophets just don't seem to have a keen sense of reality. The trumpet should be blown only if the enemy is actually at the gate. Lamentations should be heard only if there really are corpses. There was no place for an obituary in Israel's festive atmosphere. Anticipation is always dangerous.

Perhaps these were not the exact words spoken, but the inhabitants of Samaria may well have interrupted the prophet of doom with similar statements. It's even more likely, however, that they didn't bother interrupting him at all but instead smiled compassionately at this complainer bent over an imaginary coffin.

Therefore Amos continued his song of doom:

> These are the words of the Lord God:
> The city that marched out to war a thousand strong
> shall have but a hundred left,
> that which marched out a hundred strong
> shall have but ten men of Israel left (5:3 NEB).

This was the full import of the obituary, which still seemed unrealistic. Amos prophesied that a horrible military catastrophe would destroy the kingdom of ten tribes completely. That's why he could read Israel's *obituary*.

In the time of the judges, entire *tribes* went out to war. Later, in the time of the kings, the army was reorganized, and the *city* became the basis for warfare. Amos now prophesied that there would be such a frightful slaughter of the Israelites that only a hundred men would be left out of a thousand sent out by a city, while a city that sent one hundred would have only ten left. The ranks of the soldiers would literally be "decimated": nine-tenths of them would lose their lives on the field of battle. In the two world wars of our century, many young lives were lost. In the smallest villages of the countries centrally involved, the names of the fallen are listed on the church walls. Yet the slaughter of the Israelites foreseen by Amos was unique in history.

Was there no reason at all for lamentation?

The title of this chapter, "The Living Dead," sounds like the title of a detective novel or a sensational movie. It seems to refer to something unreal, but it does not. There are hundreds of living dead. The words of warning addressed to them by preachers are their funeral music, yet there is no fear in their hearts. They see their own funeral procession passing by, but they do not tremble.

Could it be that the entire church is made up of "living dead"? A quick glance at the church would lead one to say no. Some people get very angry when they hear someone suggest that the church is "dead."

No doubt the people of Israel did not like hearing that Israel was dead either. Not only was the nation healthy politically, it also seemed to be flourishing spiritually. Any visitor could see that the land was full of pilgrims, and that the songs of Zion were sung and animals sacrificed at the religious feasts. Yet, Israel was condemned to death. Even worse, it was already dead in the prophetic vision of Amos.

Amos had good reasons for writing Israel's obituary. And those reasons still exist today, for the One who is greater than Amos has written the obituary of the New Testament church: "I know all about you: how you are reputed to be alive and yet are dead" (Rev. 3:1 JB).

There is enough outward pomp and ceremony today, and there are enough festivals and memorials. We, the spiritual children of Calvin, like to speak of our fathers in proud terms. We argue about who the best Calvinists are, and we are quick to claim a place of honor in the Kingdom of Heaven. Not only do we dig the graves of our prophets when we do these things, we also build our own coffins. On our speaker's platforms we carry wreaths for our own funerals, and at our meetings we quietly fold and prepare the clothes in which we will be buried.

You are reputed to be alive — yet you are dead!

Where, amid all the loud applause, are we to find the shy blossoming of life? Where, amid all the noise and cheering, is the living testimony of Jesus Christ? Where is the tender life of prayer, and where are the ripening fruits of the inner life of faith?

When you go into the homes of certain "Christian" families, the smell of death overwhelms you as soon as you step in the door. Doesn't the anxious silence that prevails when spiritual matters are brought up remind you of the silence of the morgue?

Yet we must not generalize about such things. Then, as now, there was a "holy remnant." But in many a packed church where people have to come early if they want a place to sit, the Word of the Lord Yahweh is as startling as a thunderclap when it says: "The city that marched out to war a thousand strong shall have but a hundred left."

What will the church look like after the great sifting has taken place? "Nine-tenths of them are dead," God once said to His "chosen people." Thus, only one-tenth were alive. Did God say that *only* to Israel?

In marvellous contradiction, the prophet Amos told the virgin Israel, whose obituary he was reading and whom he already saw lying dead on the ground, to listen to what he was saying — as if a dead person could hear! This obvious impossibility did not stop Amos, for he knew that the impossible is possible with God.

For his part, he no longer expected anything of Israel, but he did expect wonders of the life-restoring *Word* of the almighty God, which he had come to proclaim. Yes, the *Word* of the Lord can create life where there is no life, if only it works fruitfully in a dead heart. If the Word creates faith, we can rely on the promise that those who believe in Christ will have eternal life.

Thus there should be sunshine — a great deal of it — in our funeral services. Those who believe in Jesus Christ but die before He returns will have to face the day when they really do hear their obituary read, when they really do see their funeral cortege moving down the street, when they really do see their coffin lowered into the grave. But *hope* breaks through the tears of the mourners. "Fallen is the virgin Israel," the solemn obituary reads. The angels respond by singing festively, "But she will rise again." "Forsaken on her land," sing the mourners below. "There is One who will raise her up," answers the chorus from above.

22.
Religion without God

Seek me and live;
but do not seek Bethel (5:4-5).

Because things seemed to be going well in Samaria, it could be argued that it was not yet time to write Israel's obituary. But there is another argument that could conceivably be used — Israel's covenant relationship with God. Many people believed that this covenant relationship excluded the possibility of Israel's destruction. The nation that had arisen from Abraham's loins was the apple of God's eye; it was His special favorite. Such a superior nation of chosen and spiritually elite people simply could not be destroyed. Because they were Abraham's descendants, the Israelites were safe. It was ridiculous to even consider the prospect of Israel's death. The heathens would have to face God's grim fury, but nothing would happen to Israel. Israel was "above" all the other nations.

The prophets, including Amos, spoke out regularly against this caricature of the covenant relationship, although they never denied the relationship as such. They simply reminded the Israelites that there are *two* parties to any covenant, and that the *condition* for Israel's life as a nation (and for eternal life in the New Testament sense) is *seeking the Lord*. God and Israel, the two parties to the covenant, could no longer walk side by side if they were not in agreement. Amos had some advice for those who loved life and enjoyed its good things: "Yahweh says this to the House of Israel: Seek me and you shall live" (5:4 JB).

Isn't that what Israel did? Didn't Israel seek the Lord? On the surface it appeared that the prophet of Tekoa could never level a more unjustified charge against the nation of the ten tribes. After all, never had the holy place which it established at Bethel been so busy. Never were so many animals sacrificed so willingly as in the time of Amos. In addition to Bethel, the people also went to Gilgal, a place regarded as intimately consecrated ever since the time of Joshua, because of the circumcisions performed there. And if that were not enough, great hosts of pilgrims regularly traveled to Beersheba. Amos himself could testify to this, for the pilgrims from the north of Israel had to pass through Tekoa. It was a long trip. It even involved going outside the boundaries of the kingdom, as we see from 5:5, which speaks of "crossing over" to Beersheba. Furthermore, Beersheba was at the very southern tip of Judah. Yet the pilgrims didn't complain about that. Wasn't Beersheba a holy place? Hadn't the Lord appeared there long ago to Isaac and Jacob? Weren't some worthy traditions connected with Beersheba?

In the light of all this, could the prophet still maintain that the Israelites did *not* seek the Lord? The religious fervor and the sacrifices and the pilgrimages certainly created an impression of spiritual health, but all this activity was part of a religion without God. God wanted nothing to do with

Bethel and Gilgal and Beersheba. That was not where He lived. He lived in His own house — and not in the houses men built for Him following their own designs. God refuses to recognize our man-made religions. They are an abomination in His eyes.

Amos draws a sharp contrast to make the judgment as harsh as possible:

> Seek me and you shall live.
> Do not seek Bethel,
> do not go to Gilgal,
> do not journey to Beersheba (5:5 JB).

Israel's pious pretence was the complete opposite of a true quest for God. At bottom it meant turning away from God. No sharper criticism could be made of our efforts to alter our religion to suit ourselves.

It may be that some Israelites tried to excuse themselves by arguing that the division of Israel into the two kingdoms made it impossible to go to Jerusalem. But even in the face of such an argument, Amos would have to maintain that holding services in Bethel, Gilgal and Beersheba did not represent a search for Yahweh. Rather, it was simple selfishness.

The entire religion of those cultic centers rested on the heathen principle that sacrifices are made to win the favor of the gods. Thus the idea in the minds of these Israelites was to make the Lord indebted to them, to harness Yahweh to the wagons of their own desires by bringing Him great offerings. The idea was not to approach the Lord's beloved countenance but to share in His gifts. That's the kind of religion they considered worthwhile. Actually, this religion was a matter of *using* God rather than of serving Him. God would serve Israel, they believed; He would feel indebted to Israel because of the many sacrifices that were brought. In short, these Israelites developed a religion without God at its center!

It's a good thing the Bible reminds us that religious fervor and religion are two entirely different things. Participation in worship services should not be equated with seeking the Lord, for the one is possible without the other. In our overflowing churches we may talk a great deal about the glory of God — without actually seeking God. There may be much activity and faithfulness to principles — but are we really seeking God? Are we perhaps mistaken in believing that we seek God? To err is human. It may well be that a pious mistake of colossal proportions has been made.

In the midst of these fervent church people so busy sacrificing and praying, we suddenly hear the harsh voice of the prophet, saying on the Lord's behalf:

> Seek *me* and live;
> but do not seek Bethel.

Those who have a low opinion of the church will perhaps find just what they're looking for in this warning given by Amos. "Listen to this!" they say. "Amos agrees with us that the important thing is seeking the Lord, and that it has nothing to do with Bethel. In other words, if you love Jesus, you don't need to go to church. 'Seek *me* — and live — but do not seek Bethel,' for the official church is as dead as a doornail." This text is then regarded as a prophetic sanction of Christianity without the church!

Before anyone is taken in by this train of thought, I must point out that its reading of Scripture is a little hasty. Its proponents should not be quite so quick to claim that God's prophet agrees with them. Did Amos say that Israel was not to seek the holiness of God's house? Of course not! All he said was that no temples were to be built in Bethel and such places, for to do so would be to construct a religion of one's own. Thus Amos condemns private religion and the unwillingness to participate in the life of the church.

Those who seek God outside the church have strayed just as far from the path as those who seek Him inside the church by way of public displays of piety. All have sinned and fallen short of the glory of God.

"Seek me and live." There are some texts that are so

well known and hang on the walls of so many homes that their meaning is in danger of being lost completely. This text from Amos is one of them. The danger is that the meaning of such texts takes a back seat to the beauty of the words. Therefore we must have a clear and detailed understanding of what it actually means to seek the Lord.

We approach such an understanding when we read what the Bible says about the death of Saul: "So Saul died for his unfaithfulness; he was unfaithful to the Lord in that he did not keep the command of the Lord, and also consulted a medium, *seeking* guidance, and did *not seek* guidance from the Lord" (I Chron. 10:13). Here seeking is equated with *asking* questions or getting advice. Seeking God means asking His advice about what we are to do. We are not just to ask once in a while when we face difficult decisions but are to come to Him *daily* to ask for guidance and strength.

In other words, we must know the Lord in all we do and must not take as much as a single step without asking, like a perplexed child, "Lord, where must I go, and what must I do?" We must seek God's approval for all our plans. It is not as though we draw up a blueprint for our life's home and ask God to become the contractor who does the actual building for us. No, we must be willing to do the building ourselves, in accordance with His instructions.

Now Amos's message starts to become real and concrete. Seek the Lord — and live! Someone who seeks God also seeks to do His *will*. Seeking God means *not* seeking evil and sin, but fleeing from them. Therefore our text reads: "Seek me, but do not seek Bethel." Seeking God means staying away from evil, or else the quest is not genuine. Seeking both God and Bethel is trying to serve both God and the golden calf. It's like trying to mix fire and water. We cannot seek God and also visit Bethel from time to time, for that would be like trying to serve both God and Mammon. Seeking God means being decisive. There is no room for fence-sitters, people torn between two opinions. We must

summon the courage to turn our backs resolutely on Bethel.
We must pluck out the eye and cut off the hand that leads to
sin. People with only one eye or one hand are regarded as
incomplete. Hence we must dare to be regarded as incomplete and imperfect.

Now the message becomes even more real and concrete.
Seek the Lord — and live! Seeking involves tension and
effort. Someone who has lost something important cannot
relax until he has found it. Those who seek God allow themselves no rest or sleep until they have found Him. Rest comes
after unrest, finding after seeking, enjoyment after effort,
relaxation after tension. That's life.

Seek the Lord and live! Those who seek God will find
rest. But those who refuse to seek God should not suppose
that the Lord will leave them at rest. If Israel refuses to seek
Yahweh, then He will seek Israel, but in a way that Israel
will not welcome. He will seek Israel in the form of a *fire* that
cannot be put out:

> Gilgal is going to be exiled
> and Bethel brought to nothing.
> Seek Yahweh and you shall live,
> or else he will rush like fire on the House of Joseph
> and burn it up, with none at Bethel able to put out the flames
>   (5:5-6 JB).

Thus nothing will be left of Bethel and Gilgal, those
beautiful centers of sacrifice. Joseph's house will go up in
flames. (This house of Joseph is the entire kingdom of the
ten tribes, which here assumes the name of its most important tribe, i.e., Ephraim, the son of Joseph.) Joseph was
Jacob's favorite son. He was the spoiled child clothed in the
coat of many colors. He was Israel, favored by God and
chosen above all nations. He was the one before whose sheaf
all the other sheaves bowed in Jeroboam's time.

And now Amos speaks of a fire that cannot be put out.
This is the tragedy of the Jews. Here we already see the
Roman soldier who throws a burning torch into the beauti-
ful temple. We see Israel as the Wandering Jew, unable to

find rest on earth.

But there is more to be seen. Through Amos's prophecy about a fire in the house of Joseph the prince, we hear the words of Jesus, who also spoke of a fire that cannot be put out, a fire into which the children of the kingdom of this earth will be thrown. That's what happens when a nation practices a religion without God.

The voice of the abandoned and forgotten God stirs us deeply as it invites Israel to seek Him and live. This is unparalleled love. What man would be so patient with a woman who had abandoned him faithlessly?

Seek the Lord and live! Why, O man, do you seek happiness as a bird in winter looks for bread on a field covered with snow? Why do you, faithless daughter and rebellious son, no longer recognize your Father in heaven? Why do you run away from Him, even though He looks after you faithfully and cannot forget you and waits anxiously for your return?

Why should you die, O house of Israel? Seek Me and live!

23.
Sinful Silence

*Therefore he who is prudent will keep silent in
such a time;
for it is an evil time (5:13).*

On the surface it appears that Amos praises this "keeping silent in an evil time" as an act of prudence. This is how commentators have usually understood this text. They have assumed that the "prudent" are those who fear God, and that the "evil time" is the moment when God punishes the wicked. Thus they explain that silence means not murmuring against God's judgment and punishment, however severe it may be; it means admitting instead that God is right, since the sins of the people are so numerous and serious. According to this way of thinking, the "silence" referred to in our text means a refusal to say anything about God's judgments;

it means sealing our lips when God's judgment strikes, in the awareness that the guilty deserve their punishment.

When we look at it this way, the "silence of the prudent" becomes a virtuous deed and an example to us. Yet, although it is a precious Scriptural truth that we must not murmur against God's judgments, this is not what Amos is talking about in this text. As the title of this chapter ("Sinful Silence") indicates, I believe that our text must be explained and applied in some other way.

This text is not about silence in the face of divine punishment at all. The word *therefore* introducing the text points back directly to the moral decay and injustice prevalent in Israel (5:12). Thus the text is talking about keeping silent in the face of *man's unrighteousness*.

Obviously Amos could not approve of such silence or regard it as exemplary. He himself protested continually against injustice. Actually, Amos himself says nothing further about whether such silence is to be condemned. That's not the issue here.

What he does here is sketch the *evils* of his time in various ways. The evil comes out in all sorts of things, including corruption and widespread lawlessness. One of the evil signs of the times, according to Amos, is that "prudent" people do not make themselves heard; wicked men and fools do all the talking. (This is a definite indication of a spiritual crisis.) Fools hold the important positions and run things, while "prudent" people withdraw from public affairs and remain silent.

Thus Amos is not saying that remaining silent is the prudent thing to do. Rather, he is reporting a sad state of affairs symptomatic of a spiritual decline: because it is an evil time, prudent people remain silent.

Those who recognize material values but not spiritual values will be surprised to hear the prosperous period when

Jeroboam II reigned referred to as an "evil time." We usually speak of an era in which there is money to be made as a "great time to be alive." In reality, of course, such a time can be exceedingly evil. If the government of the United States were to remove the words "In God we trust" from its coins, the coins would not lose their monetary value, but something would be lost all the same. Such an action would be an indication that something has gone wrong spiritually. Such a time would be an evil time. That's what Amos means.

Amos was not impressed by the wealth and beautiful palaces of Samaria, for behind the palace walls he saw ethical degeneration and spiritual sickness, despite the noise of the singing and the many sacrifices. He sketched this decay as follows:

> Trouble for those who turn justice into wormwood,
> throwing integrity to the ground;
> who hate the man dispensing justice at the city gate
> and detest those who speak with honesty.
> You have trampled on the poor man,
> extorting levies on his wheat.
> I know that your crimes are many,
> and your sins enormous:
> persecutors of the virtuous, blackmailers,
> turning away the needy at the city gate (5:7, 10, 11, 12 JB).

These words don't need much explanation. The common theme in these complaints is that justice, which is a wonderful benefit sweeter than honey, is turned into *wormwood,* which has a bitter taste and an unpleasant smell. Justice is thoroughly perverted and becomes galling injustice.

Amos goes into detail. Anyone who pleads the cause of the oppressed at the gate (the courtroom where justice was administered) is hated and abhorred. He is denounced as a *Communist* — if you'll forgive the anachronism. The capitalistic exploiters and parasites have no use for such defenders of the poor.

The wealthy knew all about exploitation. They were careful not to disobey the law that forbade demanding interest from impoverished Israelites (Ex. 22:25).* Instead, the poor farmers were pressured into giving grain. This wasn't interest, for it wasn't money: it was simply a "gift," in the form of produce, which the exploited farmer brought his "friendly" creditor. And the farmer had better be thankful, too! He should be sure to take off his hat and wipe his shoes — forgive me another anachronism — when he came to the city with his produce and knocked at the door of the mansion to report that he had come with a "present" which he hoped the "master" of the house would be kind enough to accept. "It's just a small favor," he would explain, "since the master was good enough to lend me some money."

Not only the rich but also the judges were experts in exploitation. Criminals and killers would be acquitted at once — as long as they were willing and able to pay. Money could buy anything. But the poor, who had no money in their pockets, were simply "pushed aside" when they came to the gate to have their cases heard.

This system of exploitation gave the powerful the money to indulge in such luxuries as building houses of hewn stone, which were like some of Solomon's buildings long ago. Such houses became fashionable among the powerful of Samaria. But Amos warned that they would not get much pleasure from those houses:

> You have built houses of hewn stone,
> but you shall not dwell in them;
> you have planted pleasant vineyards,
> but you shall not drink their wine (5:11).

Unfortunately, these warnings did not stop the inhabitants of Samaria from going their merry way. It was truly an evil time.

---

*This law must be seen against the background of the usury prevalent in the ancient world. In Babylon an interest of 40% was often demanded on corn that was borrowed. The general principle in the Mosaic laws is: be fair and merciful. We should also apply this principle to our "Business is business" age, although interest is not wrong in itself.

The indictment of Israel in Amos 5 is not as orderly and logical as we would expect. On the contrary, there is no real thread or continuity to be found in the prophet's words. His description of what is wrong with the people is suddenly interrupted and illuminated by a reminder about the *glory of Yahweh*. First Amos complains about turning justice into wormwood (5:7). Then he talks about the Lord as the maker of the Pleiades and Orion (5:8-9), only to return abruptly to his accusation of lawlessness. This is certainly not a logical train of thought. The prophet jumps from one thing to another, leaving us to search in vain for order in this "sermon."

Some commentators have sought a solution to this puzzle in textual criticism. They have assumed that these verses somehow were mixed up or put in the wrong place. To solve the problem, they rearranged the texts or even dropped some of them. But there is no need for such solutions. The doctrine of organic inspiration leaves plenty of room for the effect of what goes on in the mind of the prophetic author.

Someone who is stirred to the depths of his being does not speak in smooth and simple sentences. His words contain more exclamations than logical arguments. He puts in exclamation marks as he writes, but he may forget to cross a *t* here and there. We must bear in mind that the authors of the books of the Bible were often influenced by deep feelings as they wrote.

The mind of the prophet moves back and forth between the glory of Yahweh and the degeneration of Joseph. Rearranging these texts might have some advantages from a logical point of view, but we must weigh the dubious logical gain against a real loss in effect. When the prophet sees the "covenant people" sinning so grievously, his mind immediately turns to God! He cannot help injecting the thought of God into his flood of words. He is gripped by the terrible thought of people doing as they please, trampling God's laws underfoot without considering what God Himself might think or do about it.

This brings us to a second characteristic of an evil time:
There is no fear of God in the hearts of the people!

Amos gives us a beautiful picture of God:

> He who made the Pleiades and Orion,
> and turns deep darkness into the morning,
> and darkens the day into night (5:8).

We could read this as a paraphrase of the first article of the
Apostle's Creed: "I believe in God the Father, Almighty,
Maker of heaven and earth." He is the Creator, the One
who made the Pleiades and Orion, each of which is beautiful
in its own way. The Pleiades is a group of seven shining
stars that God joined together to form a holy number.
Orion's beauty is proud. With his reddish shoulder and his
twinkling foot encircled by stars, he reminds us of a mythical
titan who stormed heaven in his wild recklessness and was
chained to the earth as punishment.

As a man who spent a great deal of time outdoors,
Amos contemplated nature on the open fields of Tekoa and
read God's majesty in the pure book of His creation. He
knew God as the Maker of the Pleiades and Orion.

But God is not only the Creator. He is also the One who
maintains the creation. His daily care is reflected in the alter-
nation of day and night, light and darkness. Although the
creation of the stars strikes us as a supreme feat, the daily
upholding of creation is no less wonderful. Great is the God
who "turns deep darkness into the morning, and darkens
the day into night."

Why does Amos use *this* particular image of God? Why
does he remind us here that God created the world and upholds it? What does all of this have to do with Israel's
corruption?

Amos was interested in the *contrast*. The chosen people
were supposed to be children of God *par excellence*. Yet

how little they manifested God's image! "Look at the heavens," cried the prophet. "That's where God lives. His throne is among the stars. He is the Father of light and the Maker of the Pleiades and Orion." But the "children of light," the "cultured" city dwellers of Samaria huddled inside the walls of their palaces, contaminated and defiled themselves with sin. They had become children of darkness. Perhaps we, too, should look less at electric lights and more at the stars, less at jewelry displayed in store windows and more at the gift of time.

Amos also draws a contrast when he reminds us that God upholds the world. The fact that God upholds everything should have led the Israelites to confess humbly that the almighty Creator upholding the whole world is also "my God and Father because of Christ his Son. I trust him so much that I do not doubt he will provide whatever I need for body and soul" (*Heidelberg Catechism,* Answer 26). Instead the Israelites heaped up their ill-gotten gains.

These wayward children must not forget that this almighty God who called everything into being and upholds the whole world is also able to *destroy* and *annihilate* everything. Therefore Amos completes his sketch of God as follows:

> He summons the waters of the sea
> and pours them over the land.
> Yahweh is his name.
> He blazes out ruin on the stronghold
> and brings destruction to the fortress (5:8-9 JB).

By speaking of the waters of the sea poured out upon the surface of the earth, the prophet reminds Israel of the *flood* in Noah's time, when God opened the fountains of the great sea and poured out the waters on the surface of the earth. Would the One who commands the forces of nature be stymied by man's insignificant "culture"? Or would He decree sudden destruction for the strongholds, fortresses and beautiful palaces of Samaria?

Yet the people of Samaria paid no attention to what this powerful God had to say. It was indeed an evil time.

Now we return to our point of departure. The time was evil because of the moral degeneration and because the people did not fear God, who was to intervene in a decisive way. But the culmination of this evil was the *silence of the prudent.* Those who could still have exercised a good influence retreated fearfully into their corners.

Part of what Amos means by this "silence" is that the "prudent" ceased to demand justice for themselves. There were still plenty of people who had cases to bring to court. But they had seen often enough that the cases of the poor were simply pushed aside. If they did not bribe the judges, their cases simply wouldn't be dealt with. These upright people had too much self-respect to try to pay off a judge. Rather than subject themselves to such degrading devices, they avoided the courts altogether. "It's no use," they said to themselves. They preferred to remain silent.

This "silence" was also in part a failure to protest when others were mistreated. These "prudent" people refused to interfere or make any effort to change things, arguing that their voices would be drowned out in the tumult created by so many fools.

From a psychological point of view, this "silence" is understandable. Those who stand up for justice and truth are *hated* everywhere. Furthermore, no one seems to listen to them. Why ask for trouble and try to change things if you're bound to fail anyway?

But however understandable this silence may be, it cannot be excused. Neutral, colorless people do not escape guilt. Their silence is sinful. A person who knowingly sells stolen goods is no better than a thief. Failure to act can also be a sin. Those who trample the law underfoot are blameworthy, but those who remain silent about it are also guilty. The *Heidelberg Catechism* teaches that we become guilty of the very sins we watch in evil silence. The catechism makes this point in connection with swearing and blasphemy. The oppressors of Israel were profaning the name of God, and the silent bystanders shared in the guilt because of their failure to act. Their silence implied consent.

We have all heard the proverb "Silence is golden." There are situations where this proverb can be applied. Sometimes it is wise to be silent before God and man, but in most cases, silence is not shining gold but dark betrayal. People who speak without thinking certainly should pray that God will help them hold their tongues, for they are in danger of sinning when they speak. But sinning by remaining silent is much more common.

Today we live in an evil time — and not just in economic respects. Many fools try to give leadership in church, government and society. The rights of God and man are trampled underfoot in the streets, in courtrooms, in the chambers of government, in homes, in offices, and in factories. All kinds of apostate theories are preached openly, and decadence is promoted through books, newspapers, radio, and television.

The voice of the prudent still comes through weakly, but it does not find enough support. We let the battles rage while we sit peacefully in our living rooms and read all about it in the newspaper or watch it on the evening news. We take careful note of what's going on. We shake our heads and say, "What an evil time we live in!" Yet we show no interest in evangelism. We don't concern ourselves with the Christian labor movement or contribute money for Christian social action. We remain silent — although we are supposed to have good news for the world. We remain silent when we should be testifying. When someone comes to collect money for a Christian cause, we can't afford to contribute. We speak out loudly and boldly if our own rights are jeopardized, but when the rights and name of our God are at stake, we don't get involved.

Prudent people are silent in our time, for it's an evil time. Amos was right!

24.
Small
Dangers

It is as if a man fled from a lion,
and a bear met him;
or went into the house and leaned with his hand
against the wall,
and a serpent bit him (5:19).

Israel did not regard the "day of the Lord" as a great danger. On the contrary, the Israelites looked forward to it. Therefore Amos had to address a word of warning to those who "desire the day of the Lord" (5:18). Although such people no longer lived according to God's commandments, they still believed God was with them. They based this belief on their political and social prosperity and their victories in battle against the Syrians. They confused success with blessing, just as we do today. All their good fortune suggested to them that their future would be glorious. When the "day of

the Lord,'' which the prophets so often mentioned, finally
came, the Lord would reveal Himself further through a
complete glorification of His people and a complete annihi-
lation of their enemies. That day would bring Israel only
good and the heathens only adversity. The heathens had
every reason to fear it, but Israel had nothing to fear.

God's prophet wanted nothing to do with such idle
appeals to a one-sided covenant relationship without covenant
faithfulness. Glorying in the *benefits* of the covenant while
forgetting its *demands* was an abomination in the eyes of
Amos:

> Woe to you who desire the day of the Lord!
> Why would you have the day of the Lord?
> It is darkness, and not light (5:18).

For Amos, the *decline* of Israel was a certainty. There
would be judgment on that day. All one could hope was:

> It may be that the Lord, the God of hosts,
> will be gracious to the *remnant* of Joseph (5:15).

Only a remnant or fraction of the people would be
plucked as a brand from the burning on that day, and even
this Word of hope is introduced with ''It may be.'' In other
words, the Israelites should make haste for their own sakes
— by listening to the voice of the prophet:

> Seek good and not evil,
> that you may live,
> that the Lord, the God of Hosts, may be firmly on your side,
> as you say he is (5:14 NEB).

Once more the Israelites are told in no uncertain terms
that they must repent and be converted. Conversion is not
just a change in behavior. First and foremost it is a change
in one's attitude and thinking. The quest for the good is
praiseworthy, but it is pleasing to God only if it proceeds
from a pure soul that *loves* good and *hates* evil. Therefore
Amos has to add:

Hate evil and love good;
enthrone justice in the courts (5:15 NEB).

Amos warned the Israelites that unless they did so, their
seemingly virtuous actions would be sinful in God's eyes. In
God's name he declared:

In every public square there will be lamentation,
in every street wails of "Alas! Alas!"
Peasants will be called on to lament
as well as the professional mourners
and there will be wailing in every vineyard,
for I am going to pass through you,
says Yahweh (5:16-17 JB).

These ominous words remind us of the fearful night
when Yahweh passed through Egypt to slay the first-born in
each home. People might suppose that this would be repeated
on the "day of the Lord," that there would again be weeping
and wailing in the homes of the *heathens* and joy in *Israel*.
But such people were mistaken. The Lord would now "pass
through" His own people as He then passed through Egypt.

Amos's sketch of the misery is complete. In the cities
the dead will be so numerous that there will be wailing in
every public square and people will cry "Alas!" in *every
street*. Nor will the countryside be spared. The farmer will
be called from the field to the house where someone has
suddenly died and the professional mourners (people skilled
in lamentation) have already gathered.* Even in the vine-
yards, which are normally happy places (Judges 9:27) where
joyful songs are sung, there will be wailing. What a day that
will be!

Why, O Israel, do you regard this as such an insignificant
danger?

Using the example of the lion, the bear and the snake,

---

*On the hiring of professional mourners, see Jer. 9:17-18, Eccl.
12:5, and Matt. 9:23.

Amos gives us a vivid picture of a danger that cannot be escaped. This example may be an allusion to a certain Arab proverb about a man who fell into a pit as he fled from a bear. But it's more likely that this frightening example of danger is based on actual life (see Is. 24:18).

A man is fleeing from a lion. He has just had a terrifying encounter with the king of the beasts. He flees in fright, running as fast as he can. Because of his fear, sweat pours down his face. Running like a man possessed, he manages to escape the lion. Gasping for breath, he stops for a moment to rest. Then, right in front of him, he suddenly sees a bear! Again he faces death, and again he flees madly, with the bloodthirsty bear right behind him. He hears the beast panting for blood — human blood! Finally he can run no farther. He must stop for breath, even if it costs him his life. But then he catches sight of an abandoned shepherd's cottage. He stumbles inside and bolts the door. Exhausted, he leans against the wall·as he thinks about his narrow escape from the mouth of the lion and the claw of the bear. Now he can afford to rest after his headlong flight. He decides to stretch out on the floor. His clothes are dripping with sweat, so he takes them off. As he removes his sandals, he leans with one hand against the wall. But just where he puts his hand, there is a crack in the wall. Concealed in the crack is a small poisonous snake. The snake feels the hand and takes the man for an enemy. It bites the hand and pulls back further into the crack. The man cries out in surprise and fright. His hand swells up quickly as the poison goes to work. He turns blue, and then gray. His eyes open wide and bulge from their sockets. He dies a horrible death all by himself in the abandoned hut.

What a frightening story! The man had escaped the lion, and the bear couldn't catch him, either. But a deceptively small snake concealed in a crack in the wall carried out the death sentence, and so he died anyway. The small danger in the form of a snake simply hadn't crossed his mind. Yet it was this small danger that cost him his life.

This story is an imaginative portrayal of Israel. The nation had escaped great dangers; it had faced lions and bears. The danger of death was never far away. "I grew up with such fears and dangers," said Israel. "There were always dangers everywhere. It was a matter of 'Every man for himself.' There were the Egyptians, the Philistines, the Syrians, and so forth!"

But now Israel finally had peace, for the arm of the Lord protected him from danger. All his enemies had been defeated, and Israel could relax at last. Everyone could sleep soundly at night and go about his business calmly. There was no longer any thought of danger. "The day of the Lord? What about it? It will bring us benefits only."

Thus Israel slept. The Israelites rested calmly on the mountain of Samaria. But theirs was the false peace of death. That ancient serpent was still around. The danger the Israelites did not suspect was concealed in some wall in their own home. It was not outside, but inside.

Listen! Did you hear the small snake hiss? He'll inject his deadly poison into your body. When the day of the Lord comes, the streets will be full of corpses. People will be wailing in every public square and crying "Alas!" on all the streets.

Is it possible that you and I are not fully on guard against these "small dangers" which are actually so great? We certainly know how to defend ourselves against lions and bears. We dare take on giants. We combat apostasy and the spirit of revolution. Proudly we challenge them to do battle. We raise high the banner of Christ's kingship. The real danger is not so much that we may fall into the lion's mouth of unbelief or the claws of the Soviet bear. For that we're too well trained in the basic principles of church, state and society.

It's not so much the lion or the bear that threatens us. In fact, we see too many lions and bears along the road, and not enough snakes lurking in the corners and crevices of our own homes. That's the real problem! We must be on guard against the small snakes in the dark corners of our homes and the rooms of our hearts. The snake of our un-confessed and uncombatted sin may kill us yet! What is the snake's name? Is it Greed or Sensuality or Malice? Let's take a careful look into the cracks in our walls, before this snake gets a chance to kill us.

What do you believe concerning the day of the Lord and the return of Christ? The *Heidelberg Catechism* tells us: "All his enemies and mine he will condemn to everlasting punishment: but me and all his chosen ones he will take along with him into the joy and glory of heaven" (Answer 52). Yes, that's what I believe. But before that happens, the great killer and trampler of snakes must kill the treacherous snake of my sin through the breath of His mouth, through His Holy Spirit. Come, O Holy Spirit, and kill the small snake lodged in the wall of my home.

25.
Seasonal
Righteousness

But let justice roll down like waters,
and righteousness like an everflowing stream
(5:24).

The Israelites who lived during the time of Amos were convinced that the "day of the Lord" would mean nothing but glory for Israel. They based this conviction on their belief that Yahweh had a great deal to thank His people for. Didn't they serve Him in exemplary fashion with their sacrifices of the finest beasts and their highly organized festivals?

But now we see the prophet busy trying to show the Israelites what's wrong with their way of thinking. He does so by appealing to *history*. This approach was certain to get some response, for Israel was as sensitive to its history as a nail is to a magnet. And what a proud and glorious history it was! The Israelites glowed as they recalled the deeds of their fathers. Therefore it came as quite a blow when Amos, arguing on the basis of history, showed that the conduct of the fathers when it came to serving the Lord did not speak well for what might be expected from the children.

In the name of Yahweh, Amos asked: "Did you bring me sacrifices and gifts, you people of Israel, those forty years in the wilderness?" (5:25 NEB). The tone of the question indicates that the answer is no. Israel did not do so. Without maintaining that not a single sacrifice was offered during those forty years, Amos could and did maintain that the bringing of sacrifices — to say nothing of *overflowing* sacrifices — was very far from what it should have been.

First of all, there wasn't much to sacrifice, and secondly, there was no great desire to bring sacrifices. It's quite possible that during the long period in the wilderness, the entire practice of offering sacrifices had declined and been neglected, just as circumcision had (see Joshua 5:5-7). Whether this failure to offer sacrifices is sinful the prophet does not say — for he was not a priest — but he does use it to buttress his argument. Apparently bringing sacrifices does not have the meaning which Amos's contemporaries ascribed to it. History shows that the Lord can get along without sacrifices and does not require them as a condition for His favor. In any event, sacrifices were not offered regularly during the years in the wilderness. Yet this did not stop the Lord from leading His people to the promised land. What did the Israelites hope to achieve with all those sacrifices, anyway?

In the next verse (i.e., 5:26), Amos asks whether the Israelites had taken Sakkuth as their king and Kaiwan as their star-god.* The tone of this question also indicates that

---

*Some translations wrongly phrase this text as a statement rather than a question.

the answer must be no. The Israelites in the wilderness did not carry these two Babylonian star-gods around in processions. Sakkuth and Kaiwan — who are reminiscent of Mars and Saturn — were not yet known during the wilderness period. In the time of Amos, however, such processions did take place. Thus it looked even worse for Amos's generation.

The "fathers" in the wilderness adopted various sinful customs of the time, but Amos offers solid proof that they did abstain from two sins in which their descendants engaged. (1) They did not bring the offerings which their descendants brought in such numbers in the belief that God's favor could be *bought* through them. (2) They did not participate in the Babylonian idolatry in which their descendants became so heavily involved. Thus the fathers were completely different from the children. Therefore God would treat the children differently from the fathers. God brought the fathers *into* the promised land, but He would lead the children *out:* " 'I will take you into exile beyond Damascus,' says the Lord, whose name is the God of hosts" (5:27). *Beyond Damascus* means in the direction of Kir. That's where Sakkuth and Kaiwan lived!

After arguing on the basis of history that the Israelites were wrong in supposing that their offerings had earned them God's favor, Amos went on to tell them in precise and concrete terms what God thought of their offerings. God's criticism was devastating. As we ponder it, we should think of our own festivals, memorial services, and Sunday morning worship services with every seat occupied and the sanctuary beautifully decorated. God says:

> I hate, I despise your feasts,
> and I take no delight in your solemn assemblies.
> Even though you offer me your burnt offerings and your
>   cereal offerings,

I will not accept them,
and the peace offerings of your fatted beasts
I will not look upon.
Take away from me the noise of your songs;
to the melody of your harps I will not listen (5:21-3).

God was not beating around the bush!

When the northern kingdom established its own places for sacrifice and worship, it was careful to imitate what God had established in Jerusalem, in the belief that such imitation would please the Lord. But it's apparent that it didn't. The Lord reacted with strong language: He "hated" and "despised" their feasts. He couldn't stand the atmosphere of Bethel and Gilgal. He wanted to see and hear nothing of it. Their hymns and temple music were nothing but unwanted racket in His ears, and He was happy when they stopped for a while. Beautiful hymns were sung to Yahweh, but the music simply did not harmonize with the singing of the angels. The sacrifices of the fatted beasts disgusted Him.

Naturally Amos said nothing against sacrificing as such, for this practice was instituted by God Himself. Neither did he have anything against music, singing, organs, or harps. The music of David was pleasing to God. But if what lives in the heart does not match the beauty of the music, everything is spoiled. The perversion of the best and most beautiful things in life creates the greatest stench of all.

Taken aback, we ask ourselves what the Lord would think of our feasts and meetings. We wonder how our chorus "Glory to God in the highest" sounds in heaven. In case you haven't asked yourself this question yet, it's time you did.

Now Amos comes to something that does give the Lord great pleasure. The Lord delights in justice and righteousness so abundant that they flow like water:

But let justice roll down like waters,
and righteousness like an everflowing stream.

There are two kinds of streams in the Near East: those in which water flows only during the winter months, which is the rainy season, and those which flow both winter and summer. The winter streams contain water only when all the other streams have water as well, but the "everflowing" streams can be counted on to flow even in periods of heat and drought, when other streams have dried up.

Amos points to such an everflowing river as an example. He declares that our righteousness — in New Testament terms, our godliness — should be like an everflowing stream. We are not to be like the stream that contains water only for a little while after it rains. Our·justice and righteousness must "flow" both winter and summer. God does not ask of us a seasonal righteousness or an occasional Christianity but a permanent righteousness.

This seasonal righteousness and occasional Christianity can be found in many forms and places. Here we see a married couple who celebrate their twenty-fifth wedding anniversary by "giving thanks to the Lord" and talking about "the Lord's guidance through so many years." Yet they forget about giving to the church and do not remember that God's mercies are to lead us to *repentance*. Over there is a man who enjoys great success and speaks piously — and presumptuously — of "the Lord's blessing." But as soon as he suffers a small setback, he is ready to give up. Then there are many who put on Sunday faces as they put on their Sunday clothes. In church they sing aloud that they have a burning desire to come to the house of the Lord, when in fact they are in church only because the cold weather spoiled their plan of spending the day at the beach. There are also some who say to Jesus in apparent sincerity that they want to follow Him wherever He may lead, but they turn back when they discover that the Son of man has no place to lay His head. There are some who are happy to be on board when the church's sailboat is driven forward by favorable winds — for it makes their jobs secure or wins customers for their business — but when it's time to row against the stream, they're nowhere to be found. There are many who have courage and confidence when everyone else does, for they are like the stream that flows during the rainy season. But how few there are who sing when everyone else is crying and trust when everyone else despairs.

There are only a few of those everflowing streams that you can always rely on to contribute to Christian causes, whether they are earning a lot of money or only a little. More common is the seasonal righteousness of those who are willing to give as long as they're earning a substantial salary, but say no in times of economic hardship. The evil of seasonal righteousness is increasing.

Our righteousness should be like an everflowing stream. What a joy it is to meet one of those everflowing Christians who never disappoint you, not even in times of great drought. The great contrasts of life (rain and drought, abundant harvests and years of famine, health and sickness, riches and poverty) do not destroy their faith and trust, for they know that all these things come to them from God's fatherly hand.

There is a great danger facing us here. We are still living in a "season" of common grace, in which God makes our life and the life of the church possible. One day will come the terrifying season of great heat or great cold (depending on how you look at it), the season of the Antichrist, when no one will be able to buy or sell unless he exchanges the seal of the Spirit for the mark of the Beast. There are many for whom that awful time will prove too much. If they trust in peace and order, what will they do when the Jordan floods?

Woe to the man who does not repent on time and turn from seasonal righteousness to permanent righteousness!

For all of us, who stumble every day and stray from the path we are to follow, it is a great joy to know that despite man's unfaithfulness, God is ever faithful. He will give us relief even in the most extreme heat.

26.
Fear That Came Too Late

And if ten men remain in one house, they shall die. And when a man's kinsman, he who burns him, shall take him up to bring the bones out of the house, and shall say to him who is in the innermost parts of the house, "Is there still any one with you?" he shall say, "No," and he shall say, "Hush! We must not mention the name of the Lord" (6:9-10).

The sixth chapter of Amos is typical of the book's great beauty and power. In this chapter the prophet draws on various resources of human language, such as irony, humor, puns, aphorisms and quotations, to shake the people out of their false optimism. He begins with a bit of irony.

Woe to those who are at ease in Zion,
and to those who feel secure on the mountain of Samaria,*

---

*Here Amos mentions both Judah and the kingdom of the ten tribes. Thus, although the prophet addresses most of his words to Israel alone, in this passage he is speaking to the entire covenant people.

the notable men of the first of the nations,
to whom the house of Israel come! (6:1).

Here Amos addresses himself to the elite of Israel, the ones
"to whom the house of Israel come," i.e., the common
people with their legal problems and the poor farmers with
their rent. These "notable men" were the judges and the
wealthy who flaunted their riches. They were the nobility of
Israel, but they were certainly not noble in spirit. They were
supposed to be the cream of the crop, but they were actually
brutes, trampling the poor and defenseless underfoot. They
lived in luxury, but they could only spare a few pennies for
the collection plate.

Amos speaks mockingly of these brutes as the "notable
men" of "the first of the nations"! Israel was indeed the
"first of the nations," as the Israelites like to put it in those
days. Israel was the leading nation, the superrace, the cream
of the crop! Israel was the people chosen by Yahweh; Israel
was the darling of the gods. It was the noblest of races and
the greatest of blessings to mankind. Israel threw its weight
around and asked, "Who dares take me on?" Was it not
crystal clear that this nation enjoyed God's special favor?
Had He not blessed Israel in battle in recent years? Wasn't
Israel the greatest power in Palestine? Even if some neighboring nation were bold enough to attack Israel, there were
still the great strongholds. The Israelites could rely completely on Zion and feel perfectly safe behind the strong
walls of Samaria. This was the attitude of the elite members
of this elite nation who lived in Zion and felt secure on the
mountain of Samaria.

Amos continues in an even more scornful way:

Make a journey to Calneh and look,
go on from there to Hamath the great,
then down to Gath in Philistia.
Are they any better off than these kingdoms?
Is their territory larger than yours? (6:2 JB).

We sense the irony when we realize that the three cities named here, i.e., Calneh, Hamath and Gath, were not major cities at all. The name *Hamath the great* must be taken with a grain of salt. These cities were the capital cities of some of the tiny kingdoms between Egypt and Mesopotamia. But in the land of the blind, a man with one eye is king. Israel was a true Gulliver among these Lilliputians!

Israel gloried in its position. Among these small kingdoms it was a power to be reckoned with and was addressed in respectful terms. It was the boss.

Israel acted like a small town competing with other small towns, contesting their claims to fame and glory. This led to the making of songs, which were probably soldiers' songs used to celebrate the glories of Israel's dominance over these tiny kingdoms, just as the fans of a college football team sing that their team cannot be beaten. Such songs were sung during the time of Amos, and he quotes from one of them:

> Make a journey to Calneh and look,
> go on from there to Hamath the great,
> then down to Gath in Philistia.

According to this "national hymn," there was no kingdom on earth as great as Israel. The prophet now joins in sarcastically by quoting this song. He then asks:

> Are they any better off than these kingdoms?
> Is their territory larger than yours? (6:2 JB).

Israel had certainly become great. Not one of the tiny kingdoms dared attack it — not "powerful" Calneh, not "Hamath the great," not gigantic "Gath." Israel had come a long way!

But — there was still the great power Assyria, the giant that the prophet never mentions specifically but always keeps in mind. Assyria, a nation that easily swallowed up small kingdoms, was not regarded as a danger by Israel, for its statesmen simply couldn't see that far. But Amos, with his prophetic vision, could see Assyria coming. He warned:

> You shall head the column of exiles;
> that will be the end of sprawling and revelry (6:7 NEB).

Even in this warning of the punishment to come, Amos used irony. Israel claimed to occupy a position at the head of all nations. Later it would get what it deserved: a place at the head of the column of exiles! The Israelites were used to being first. Well then, they would be first in the great deportation. They would march in the front ranks of the exiles. The "first" would truly be first!

The judgment was not announced without good reason. The indictment read as follows:

> You think to defer the day of misfortune,
> but you hasten the reign of violence.
> Lying on ivory beds
> and sprawling on their divans,
> they dine on lambs from the flock,
> and stall-fattened veal;
> they bawl to the sound of the harp,
> they invent new instruments of music like David,
> they drink wine by the bowlful,
> and use the finest oil for anointing themselves,
> but about the ruin of Joseph they do not care at all (6:3-6 JB).

We have already heard this refrain more than once, but Amos was not simply repeating himself. There are two things brought to the fore as particularly blameworthy and deserving of punishment: decadence and profane practices.

Amos draws a sharp contrast when he says that the Israelites defer the day of misfortune (i.e., the day of the Lord's judgment) but hasten the reign of violence. This shows us what was going on in the palaces of the rich, those dens of iniquity. The total impression we get is one of decadence, of a culture that mistakenly thinks itself superior.

The customs and ethos of Israel's forefathers were radically uprooted and cast aside. In itself this was not so serious, but it was a sign of something deeper. Everything was geared toward greater enjoyment and sensual pleasure. Instead of following the traditional custom of "sitting" at the table (see Judges 19:6, I Sam. 20:5, and I Kings 13:20), the new style was to lie on couches to eat, which seems to be a lazy way to live. It may be that lying on couches is easier and more hygenic. This custom may be unobjectionable in itself, but it certainly does have a worldly flavor.

The same could be said of the way meat was used and eaten. In an earlier age, meat was eaten only on feast days. In Solomon's time, meat was eaten daily at the *court*. In Amos's day, ordinary citizens wanted to do the same. With their refined taste, they chose the very best: the choicest cuts of lamb and the finest veal. They raised their living standards and enjoyed refined luxuries.

Still worse were the profane practices, the desecration of the holy in which many people participated. The noise they made to the accompaniment of the harp, an instrument that naturally reminded them of David, clearly illustrates this. David's beautiful temple music was imitated in dinner concerts arranged to entertain Israel's leaders at their great drinking parties. While David used his talent to serve the Lord, they used their talents for sensual purposes. Even the words Amos uses make us think of some sort of bizarre combination of instruments strongly reminiscent of a modern jazz band.

Amos's complaint becomes still clearer when he accuses the Israelites of drinking wine by the bowlful. Even a moderate drinker can object to the excessive consumption of alcohol, but Amos's main concern was not the quantity of wine consumed but the bowls used to drink it. Although he does not say so explicitly, he leaves the impression that the bowls used were the "holy bowls" intended solely for use in the temple. What the heathen king Belshazzar did in his crude pride during the time of the exile was already anticipated by the covenant people before the exile.

Do you begin to see why Israel had to go into exile? What they did with the wine they also did with oil. Amos complains that they anointed themselves with the finest oils, by which he probably means that they profaned the holy oil reserved for special purposes. This oil used in joy would bring them misery. Great would be their sorrow.

Our text for this chapter paints a horrible picture of the suffering that awaited Israel. Amos shows us the city of Samaria at a time when the Lord passed through it with His fearful judgments. We are shown a house occupied by a family of ten, all of whom were stricken by some plague or other. One of them has just died, and a relative — probably an uncle — enters the house accompanied by a "burner."

The presence of this companion is already a horrible thought, for burning the bodies of the dead was considered an abomination in Israel. But when a dangerous epidemic spread through the land, such measures as burning corpses became necessary for public health reasons. Therefore the uncle comes with someone to burn the body. But as they enter this home, they are appalled at what they find: there is not just one body to be taken away and burned, but many. The dead are still stretched out on their couches, their vacant eyes wide open. The corpses are the faded color of death. The two men feel the stench of death in their nostrils. How many are still alive? Suddenly they are silenced by a sound from the back of the house. The uncle cries out, "Who's that? Is there anyone else alive besides you?" The solitary survivor responds with a weak voice, for the deadly disease has taken its toll of his body as well. "Not one," he says.

What a chilling scene! But as soon as the uncle hears this answer, he says, "Be quiet!" He thinks to himself, "This situation is too horrible for the name of Yahweh to be mentioned." If the survivor were to elaborate on his misery, he might mention God's holy name. He might start praying. Therefore the uncle says, "Be quiet! Don't mention the name of Yahweh."

This was a manifestation of an idolatrous heathen idea that had penetrated into Israel, namely, that mentioning the

name of one of the gods would draw the attention of that
god. In this particular case that would be fatal, for if Yahweh
heard someone mention His name, He would come quickly
and kill those who were still alive. The uncle, deathly afraid
of losing his own life, sternly commands the suffering survivor in the back of the house to remain silent: "Don't say
anything. Don't pray. Don't mention that fearful name. Be
quiet. Don't say a word."

What moves the uncle to ask for silence is neither the
majesty of death nor any desire to show his respect through
silence. The uncle is afraid. He is gripped by a deadly fear of
Yahweh. He is so afraid that he does not dare mention
Yahweh's name, and is just as afraid to hear anyone else
mention it.

Things can change. There have also been times when
people have been very free in their use of the name of
Yahweh. Jesus' warning to those who cry "Lord! Lord!"
was not without reason. In songs of triumph and in hymns
sung in the temple, the name of Yahweh was used boldly
and frequently. In short, people spoke of God in a very
familiar way. Some even looked forward to the "day of the
Lord."

Yet, hardly does the day of the Lord arrive for them
than their familiarity becomes a deadly fear. Those who once
mentioned the name of the Lord freely no longer dare take
it upon their lips.

Only something earthshaking could turn such a generation into God-fearing people. Yet the fear of God that results from such an event is the wrong kind of fear. It arises
not from love for God but from anxiety about what He
might do to us. Furthermore, this fear comes too late. If
Amos's preaching had taught the people a genuine fear of
the Lord, it would no longer be necessary to be afraid. The
"day of the Lord" need not reduce us to anxious silence. It
is a time for praying to Yahweh, the God of life! It is good
for us to remain silent as we listen to this frightening Word

of God, so that we will not be struck dumb with fearful anxiety when we face the day of the Lord.

The name of the Lord is also used very freely today. We use it in our prayers, in our preaching, in our arguments, at festivals, at a deathbed, in all sorts of situations. Aren't we a bit too familiar with God? Let us pray that the Holy Spirit will change our familiarity with the Lord into a true fear of the Lord, so that ours will not be a fear that came *too late.*

27.
Lo-debar and Karnaim

You who rejoice in Lo-debar (a thing of naught), who say, "Have we not by our own strength taken Karnaim (horns) for ourselves?" (6:13).

Again and again Amos attacks the rich. He lashes out against the nobles and the wealthy with his cutting words. The "palaces," those dens of iniquity and dissolute living, are an abomination to him. He warns that they will be consumed by God's lightning.

Yet the prophet was not a defender of the proletariat or a Marxist preaching against "capitalism." The rich are evil not because they are rich but because they are godless. The poor are no better, though. They may be guilty of different sins, but their sins are no less serious. The poor suffer from the same unspiritual mentality as the rich. The rich and the poor are equally materialistic, even though the former seem

to have everything, while the latter rarely enjoy anything of
"the fat of the land." Therefore, when God's great day of
judgment comes, the hovels of the poor will be destroyed
together with the palaces of the rich.

> For behold, the Lord commands,
> and the *great house* shall be smitten into fragments,
> and the *little house* into bits (6:11).

God will bring this about because the Israelites had
turned the moral order upside down. They were to reap
what they had sown. This is what Amos is getting at in the
next verse:

> Do horses run upon rocks?
> Does one plow the sea with oxen?
> But you have turned justice into poison
> and the fruit of righteousness into wormwood (6:12).

On first reading, this text seems to make little sense.
Horses can run, but not upon rocks, and one can plow with
oxen, but not upon the sea. Yet the Israelites apparently
thought they could do such absurd things, for they turned
justice into poison and the fruit of righteousness into wormwood. This was a fatal mistake, for just as horses cannot
run on rocks or oxen walk on water, injustice is no basis for
the state and society.

This mistake is another reason for judgment. The horses
that run on rocks will be smashed, and the oxen will drown
in the sea. Israel will likewise be destroyed because it does
such crazy things. What are those horses doing on the rocks?
What are those oxen doing on the sea? Why is Israel turning
everything upside down? Things were bound to go wrong!

The sinner does not agree instantly with the logic of
this argument — the sinner is never logical — and does not
forsake his path of sin. No, the sinner gives the prophet no
reason to believe that he has changed his attitude and ways.
On the contrary, Amos notes a vain boasting and a childish
pleasure in trivial things.

He expresses this in a sentence translated as follows in

the King James version: "Ye which rejoice in a thing of naught, which say, Have we not taken to us horns by our own strength?" When we read.the text this way, its meaning is far from clear. We wonder just what is meant by this "thing of naught." The question "Have we not taken to us horns by our own strength?" also leaves us completely in the dark. We've heard of wearing horns because of stupidity, but getting horns through "strength" is somewhat mysterious. Yet the meaning of the text quickly becomes clear if the words which the King James version translates literally as "a thing of naught" and "horns" are left untranslated. The Hebrew words are *Lo-debar* (a thing of naught) and *Karnaim* (horns). This suddenly casts an interesting light on the situation. The text then reads:

> You rejoice over Lo-debar,
> "Was it not by our own strength," you say,
> "that we took Karnaim?" (6:13 JB).

Instead of "a thing of naught" and "horns," we suddenly have the *names* of two places east of the Jordan. They were not the very smallest towns in the area, but neither were they of great importance. The one town had been given the name *Lo-debar,* which means *not much.* Perhaps jealous inhabitants of another town in the area had given it this name as a joke. The other town bore the name *Karnaim.*

The names of these towns occur elsewhere in Israel's history. We read about Lo-debar in II Samuel 9:4-5 and 17:27. Lo-debar was the home of Machir, the son of Ammiel, who for some time hid Mephibosheth, the son of Jonathan. And in Genesis 14:5 we read: "Chedorlaomer and the kings who were with him came and subdued the Rephaim in Ashteroth-*karnaim.*" This is no doubt the same Karnaim mentioned in our text.

The Israelites now boasted about these two places, Lo-debar and Karnaim. Why? Were they such famous cities? Were they cities known the world over? Not at all. In fact, they were two insignificant towns in Gilead.

In a war against the Syrians, Jeroboam II had seized part of the land east of the Jordan from the Aramaeans. These two towns then fell into the hands of the "victorious" army. Taking these towns was not a major triumph, but in the less glorious days of later generations, small victories were turned into great triumphs, so that there would always be *something* to boast about. The more they talked about this "mighty" military achievement, the more their national pride and collective imagination turned this conquest into an event of immense historical importance. If the Israelites of Amos's day had been Germans, they would surely have established a memorial or "Denkmal" there: "Over here, ladies and gentlemen, we have the Lo-debar Memorial, and there you see the Karnaim Memorial."

Amos merrily turns it into a joke. You who rejoice in Lo-debar, why don't you boast about the might that conquered Karnaim while you're at it?

> "For behold, I will raise up against you a nation,
> O house of Israel," says the Lord, the God of hosts;
> "and they shall oppress you from the entrance of Hamath
> to the Brook of the Arabah" (6:14).

Where are the generals and officers who conquered Lo-debar and Karnaim? They're at the head of the column of exiles. Where are the heroes whom we praised to the skies? They're in prison.

This kind of vain praise is not foreign to modern man, nor is it unknown in the twentieth century church. Who doesn't glory secretly or openly in a medal or citation for bravery won at Lo-debar or Karnaim? Haven't we *earned* our medals? And yet we confess in church that our best works in this life are imperfect and stained by sin. That's the *doctrine* of the church. Yet *life* seems to make other demands. We take pride in the glorious events in the history of our church. Are we not the purest manifestation of the Body of Christ? Have we not come a long way from our humble beginnings as a church? We cannot help but think of the struggles of our forefathers during the Reformation era. Yet in church we sing that these things are not our own doing but the work of God's hand. That's also what Israel sang. Similarly, we claim that we're not interested in glorifying the generals and officers of Lo-debar and Karnaim, or making saints of Luther and Calvin. To God be the glory!

After we have said all these things, we return to the order of the day and try to build ourselves up by boasting about Lo-debar and Karnaim. We debate such questions as who is the greatest hero of all and who carried out his duties most faithfully. Soon we, too, are ready to erect "memorials" at Lo-debar and Karnaim.

What was it the apostle said? "So what becomes of our boasts? There is no room for them" (Rom. 3:27 JB). There is no room for boasting, for our blessings are unearned.

But I will have to halt this train of thought here. Was our fight at Lo-debar and Karnaim in vain?

Those who enjoy boasting should boast about the Lord!

28.
The Background

O Lord God, forgive, I beseech thee! (7:2).

The Bible allows us many a glimpse of the background of events. Amos 7 shows this in a surprising way as it gives us some insight into Amos and his preaching.

First we are shown the background of his preaching. We have heard Amos declare repeatedly and unequivocally that Israel will fall. There is no thought of revoking the punishment. How does the prophet know this? How does he dare speak of judgment in such a bold and uncompromising way? He tells us: "This was what the Lord God showed me" (7:1 NEB).

With these words the prophet introduces a new section that begins with chapter 7. He tells us of five *visions* in which the judgment awaiting Israel is presented in symbolic form. The judgment is now made concrete and vivid.

There is a clear progression in this somber series of visions. In the first two visions, i.e., the swarm of locusts and the fire (7:16), the light of grace is still present. The Lord relents and declares, "It shall not be." But in the following three visions, i.e., the plumb line (7:7-9), the basket of summer fruit (8:1-3), and the destruction of the altar (9:1), the judgment is irrevocable.

These visions form the *background* of Amos's preaching. It is because the Lord showed him these things that he is so certain of what he says. He was only proclaiming what he had seen with his own eyes. The loud cry of judgment mirrors what Amos saw in his visions.

We are also given some idea of how Amos felt when he became aware of these irrevocable judgments of God. The Bible reveals not only what Amos did in his office as prophet but also what went on in the depths of his soul. We see that the *office* is not the alpha and the omega, for the personality, piety and prayer of Amos as a *human being* are also very important.

Because of his office, the prophet had to say some very unpleasant things to his people. Again and again he demanded repentance, heaping one judgment upon another. It almost appears that Amos acquired a kind of expertise in breaking bad news, and that he felt at home with talk of thunder and lightning. His stare was rigid and harsh. The words fell from his lips like hammer blows. Did the prophet have a heart? Was he a man of flesh and blood? Did he perhaps take pleasure in announcing the judgments to come?

The very first vision, that of the locusts, already answers these questions. This vision shows us the inner side of his prophetic personality. It tells us what kind of impact God's assignment made on him, how it affected him, and how he felt about it.

The prophet Amos did not speak to his contemporaries solely about his own experiences. His task was not just to testify to what he personally had lived through. Such subjective preaching would not have done the Israelites any good. His assignment was to bring them God's Word. This meant presenting facts and realities. Amos was faithful to his commission. On the other hand, he did not hide his own experiences timidly in the folds of his prophetic garments. He did not assume that his personal reaction was of no concern to anyone. He did not subscribe to the view that the personality of the preacher must bow before the glory of the office. On the contrary, he boldly bared his soul and revealed how he wrestled in prayer to save his people when the Lord showed him Israel's coming destruction in the vision of the locusts:

> This is what the Lord Yahweh showed me:
> it was a swarm of locusts
> at the time when the second crop was starting to grow,
> a swarm of full-grown locusts, when the king's cutting was over.
> They were about to devour all the greenstuff in the land,
> but I said, "Lord Yahweh, forgive, I beg you.
> How can Jacob survive, being so small?"
> And Yahweh relented;
> "This shall not happen," said Yahweh (7:1-3 JB).

This is a beautiful and tender scene. The farmer from Tekoa is in his house, in the room in which he prays. When he sees what is to befall his people, the prophet of doom becomes a priest interceding for them. The clenched fists become hands folded in prayer. Amos, we'll learn to love you yet!

We thought he could do nothing but preach judgment, but now it turns out that he can pray, too. It looked as though he could only play one weary tune on his harp, namely, the song of Israel's destruction, but now he uses all the strings in the harp of his soul in a mighty prayer of intercession to Israel's covenant God. It looked as though prophesying doom was easy to for him, but now we see what a burden it must have been. Full of fear, he prays, "O Lord, save us!" Before his people he appears as a somber prophet of judgment, but before God's countenance he kneels in the dust as a high priest interceding for others. To Israel he says, "What you face is judgment. It's too late for forgiveness." To God he says, "O Lord God, forgive, I beseech thee!" With biting irony he cries out in Samaria's streets, "Joseph, Joseph, you're really something. There isn't a kingdom that dares to attack you." But while praying in his inner room he cries out, "O Lord, what will Jacob be after this?" In God's name he prophesies, "Israel, get ready to meet God. Tell your complaints to Him, if you dare." But in his inner room he asks in prayer, "How can Jacob survive, being so small?"

This is a glorious paradox. Amos is both prophet and priest. He threatens and pleads. He brings God's message to man, but his troubled soul also has a message for God. On the one hand we see Amos in his office as prophet, and on the other hand we see him as a person. Happy the church with a minister who can both preach and pray! Happy the church that *knows* that its preacher is alo a priest.

This prayer reveals even more of the background of Amos's preaching. "O Lord God, forgive, I beseech thee!" What was Amos talking about? He saw a swarm of locusts. In Palestine this meant a major catastrophe. The harvest would be ruined and the people plunged into poverty. Amos tells us explicitly that *the Lord* made the swarm of locusts: "Thus the Lord God showed me: behold, he was forming locusts" (7:1). Amos was not, then, talking about a natural disaster. In our time we explain all such catastrophes on the basis of natural, economic and social causes. And then we protest against the locusts that rob us of our produce. But Amos believed that leaves and grass, harvests and drought, locusts and ravaged lands are not the result of chance or impersonal natural processes but come to us from God's fatherly hand, which not only blesses us but also chastises us. *God* formed the swarm of locusts.

This plague began when the second crop was beginning to sprout. It happened in the spring, then, after the "king's early crop" had already been harvested by his servants. The king had a right to the "early crop," the first luxuriant growths, which were used in the royal stables. Claiming this crop was his way of collecting taxes on the land. Thus the king's harvest was already safe in his barns — just in time.

This sort of thing happens often in times of poverty. The rich manage to get by, for they have something put away for a rainy day. They may complain the most, but they are the ones least affected by the crisis. This leads the revolutionary to shake his fist at the rich, but the believer remains silent. He thinks of what Jesus said about the birds of the air and the lilies of the field. He ponders Jesus' statement that it is very difficult for a rich man to enter the kingdom of heaven.

The king had already taken his harvest from the field. The hopes of the little man and the farmer were fixed on the second crop, which was to be harvested a little later. But before the second crop was ripe, a swarm of locusts suddenly appeared. The prophet, who saw all this in his vision, was beside himself with fear and cried out, "What if they devour all the crops growing on the land?" The damage would be incalculable. Therefore he intervened — through prayer.

It is obvious that this vision of the army of locusts also symbolizes other armies — enemy armies — that would come later and plunder the countryside until it was barren, trample the people underfoot, and lead Israel into captivity. The imaginary judgment symbolizes the destruction of the people of Israel.

What strikes me especially is the content of Amos's prayer: "O Lord God, forgive, I beseech thee!" He immediately went into the *background* of the catastrophe. Although he did not forget about the locusts devouring the crops, he was aware that there was more to this catastrophe. Therefore he prayed for *forgiveness*.

This was an amazing cry of distress. It would have been much more natural for Amos to pray, "Lord, please take those locusts away! Don't let them devour our crops. Think what that would mean." That's how we pray! Our primary concern is that the locusts and anything else standing in the way of our prosperity be removed immediately. Once the obstacles are gone, we laugh once more, just as Pharaoh did, and harden our hearts.

But that was not Amos's way. The misery and distress he saw were much worse than any plague of locusts. What filled him with fear was not the swarm of insects but the spiritual decay that had long ago robbed Israel of its purity. What Amos feared was sin! Behind all the problems and plagues of our time is the guilt of the world and the church. With his prophetic eye, Amos immediately saw this judgment as a result of Israel's *guilt*. Therefore he did not pray for the removal of the plague, nor did he mutter, "How do these locusts dare to attack God's chosen people?" All he did was pray simply, "O Lord God, forgive, I beseech thee!"

When will *we* ever learn that our sin is the cause of the world's problems? I'm not asking when we'll agree with this in theory — for we did that long ago. I'm asking when it will lead us to cry out to God in prayer, "O Lord God, forgive, I beseech thee!" When will *we* learn to be bothered by the sins nibbling away at the crops planted in our souls? When will *we* learn to be troubled by the locusts that devour all that is good in our lives and leave us impoverished? When will *we* learn to *pray*? O Lord, teach me, a poor fool, how to pray!

Amos's prayer was heard because it was a genuine prayer pleasing to God. The Lord listened to Amos, who was weeping not over a harvest lost to the locusts but over a people lost in sin. It was not the extent of the crisis but its cause that terrified Amos. He based his plea on the proper grounds. He did not try to say anything on his people's behalf. All he could say was that Jacob is *small*, a pitiful refugee, a lonely wanderer. He asked God to have pity on Jacob.

But this request that God be merciful to Jacob was not a last, desperate appeal or a shot in the dark. On the contrary, in this prayer Amos based himself on the granite foundation of the *covenant*. He appealed to Yahweh as the God of the covenant and the oath. He appealed to the God of Jacob!

The Lord has no name more beautiful than *God of Jacob*. That He is the God of Abraham can easily be understood, for we think of Abraham as a major figure in the Kingdom of Heaven. Abraham walked before God's countenance and was righteous. But Jacob tried to flee from God's presence and was unrighteous. We feel a much closer affinity to the worrying and struggling Jacob than to Abraham.

That God is willing to link His glorious name with the sinful name of Jacob is a great comfort to us, particularly because the name of Jacob reminds us of the covenant God made with our *fathers*. Calvin points out that there is nothing more likely to make God take pity on us than appealing to the covenant of grace. "And if we sometimes through weakness fall into sins, we must not therefore despair of God's mercy, nor continue in sin, since baptism is a seal and indubitable testimony that we have an eternal covenant with God."*

Thus God heard the prayer of Amos. "The Lord relented and said, 'This shall not happen' " (7:3 NEB). We should not get sidetracked into discussing the mysteries of God's seemingly human characteristics, nor should we debate the question whether it makes sense to speak of God changing His mind. Rather, we should glory in God's wonderful willingness to alter His plans, just as we glory in His massive resolution to abide by the covenant He has made with man.

We must remember that prayer enables the little man — Amos was also a little man — to persuade God to lay aside the rod and release streams of blessing from the source of life. Through prayer we may even persuade Him to close the gates of hell and open the gates of heaven.

That's what happened when Amos prayed. That's also how our great High Priest, who is much greater than Amos, prays. Lord, teach us how to pray!

---

*Quoted from the form for the baptism of infants used in the Christian Reformed Church.

29.
The Sagging Wall

He showed me: behold, the Lord was standing beside a wall built with a plumb line, with a plumb line in his hand (7:7).

After the spring vision of the locusts, Amos saw a summer vision, that of the glowing fire that consumed the earth and dried up the waters under the earth (7:4-6). He tells us that this fire "devoured the great deep and was eating up the land."

This vision contains the same kind of lesson as the vision of the locusts. The only difference is that the position of unrepentant Israel has become even more precarious. Thanks to the intercession of Amos, the locusts did not get far in their destructive work. But in the summer's heat of the second vision, a great deal of damage has already been done, and the prayer of the prophet succeeds only in preventing *complete* ruin. The storm of God's judgment was getting much closer. This is also apparent from the third vision, to which we now turn our attention.

The Lord's own explanation of this vision makes it clear that He will *no longer* overlook the sins of His people and let them go unpunished. The measure is full, and the judgment will not be revoked. Therefore the prophet is no longer allowed to *intercede* for his people. (This is what makes the vision of the plumb line such a somber matter.) At the start, when the locusts came, the Lord was still willing to forgive, and He continued to be forgiving when the fire broke out. But the time for forgiveness is over. Intercession is no longer possible!

Therefore this vision is the most frightening of the three, even though it contains no dangerous animals or insects and no fire. All it contains is a carpenter's tool. What was it that Amos saw? "He showed me: behold, the Lord was standing beside a wall built with a plumb line, with a plumb line in his hand."

For the people of the ancient Near East, the *wall* was the same as the city itself. When the exiles prayed to God to restore Jerusalem, they asked that its *walls* be rebuilt. And when the Lord threatened to destroy a city, He said, "I will send a fire upon its *wall.*" Thus when Amos mentions a wall in the vision, we are to think of a city, namely, Israel's capital city, which represents the heart of the entire country. Thus the wall represents Israel as a nation; it symbolizes the Old Testament church.

Amos tells us that this wall was built originally with a plumb line. In other words, the wall was built properly. God had not established Zion as a shapeless pile of stones. Jerusalem was well built. Those who looked at her could recognize the hand of the Builder. Speaking in spiritual terms, we could say that the Lord had given His people the purest ordinances for church, state and society. Everything was in holy order. Everything was directed toward one goal: the glory of God. God had given Israel the benefit of His statutes and ordinances. He has done the same for the church of the new covenant, which is built squarely on the foundation of the apostles and prophets, with Jesus Christ as its chief cornerstone.

There are people who don't like to hear about order and structure, doctrine and discipline. They want nothing to do with a plumb line and don't believe in church *walls*. But there's no getting around it: the wall was built with a plumb line!

The Lord now appears at the wall. He has a plumb line in His hand. This in itself is a disturbing thought. In the days when the Bible was written, an inspector would check the walls of old buildings and fortifications to see whether they were sagging and slanted. If there was any danger of collapse, if a wall was leaning too much, an irrevocable judgment would be pronounced: the wall would have to come down.

When God said, "Look, I am going to measure my people Israel by plumb line" (7:8 JB), this meant not that He was carrying out a judgment but that He was preparing for judgment. No one uses a plumb line to *tear a wall down*. It was used only to determine whether a wall was sagging so badly that the only thing to do was to tear it down. That was what would happen to the wall of Israel.

Just as a wall was built with a plumb line and later checked with a plumb line, so the Lord ordered everything in Israel according to His laws. Israel was to be measured by those ordinances! Now then, the Lord arrived on the scene to do some checking. He had a plumb line in His hand. Could there be anything wrong with the wall? Amos knew the answer all too well. He knew that Israel's life had become a chaotic mess.

Thus we can understand the prophet's fear when he answered the question "What do you see, Amos?" by saying, "A plumb line." Amos didn't say anything about the wall, and he didn't mention the Lord. All he saw was the plumb line. It was the plumb line that frightened him, for he realized that the Lord was about to check up on His people.

Amos knew only too well that the checking would lead to *judgment*. The wall would have to be *pulled down*. He knew those walls thoroughly, for he had stood on them to voice his complaints and accusations. He had seen the ethical degeneration. He had observed the people at Bethel with their man-made religious ceremonies. He had thundered against the perversion and violation of the law. He had wept at the religious hypocrisy. And now it was too late, for the Lord appeared on the scene with a plumb line in His hand. The wall of disobedience and shame and murmuring would not be left standing. Not one stone would be left upon another. The time for mourning had come!

What would happen if the Lord were to visit you and me with a plumb line in His hand? Are you and I living up to our callings? Are we still what the Lord wants us to be — a city set on a hill? Is it possible that our disobedience has caused the wall of our church, our home or our heart to sag much more than we suspected? Could it be that the wall is more run down and riddled with cracks than we thought? What will the Lord think of our wall of disobedience? Let's inspect those walls ourselves and own up to what's wrong with them.

Then there's the wall of the *church*. We're proud of our church. Its walls are straight and even. Our church is the purest manifestation of the Body of Christ. We think of ourselves as watchmen on Zion's walls. You should come once and admire our church walls. But don't look through the windows at what goes on behind the walls. And don't look into the room where our church council meets, where there seems to be little place for the word *brother*. Otherwise you may have the same experience the prophet Ezekiel had when he was told to dig a hole in the wall of the temple: the more he dug, the more abominations he found! There are certainly abominations to be found in our church. There is ecclesiastical pride. There is little brotherly feeling and love. There is selfishness disguised as piety. There is materialism, jealousy, and quarreling. Woe to us if the Lord should come to inspect the walls of our church!

And then there are the walls of our family! We're skilled at hiding the cracks and splits. We paper over everything with a facade. Those who look in from the outside don't see how run-down and dilapidated the walls really are.

But that won't fool the Lord! He also investigates this wall with His plumb line. He knows the state of your marriage, what your relationship to your children is, and how your children get along with each other.

He also sees the crooked paths you take at work or in your business. He observes everything that people do. He knows how we cheat on our income tax returns, although we learned how to silence our consciences on that score long ago. He knows how we scheme politically — under the banner of Christian politics. The Lord knows all about it.

Woe to us when He comes to inspect our walls and notes all that has gone wrong. "Look," He says, "I am going to measure my people Israel by plumb line." There's no use hoping that He'll forget to look inside, or that something might escape His attention. *Everything* will be checked carefully. As His yardstick, He will use the plumb line of His pure law.

When God checks our walls, He will be forced to condemn them to destruction. That's what happened to Israel.

The high places of Isaac are going to be ruined,
the sanctuaries of Israel destroyed,
and, sword in hand, I will attack the House of Jeroboam (7:9 JB).

It should not escape our attention that the Lord speaks of *Isaac's* high places. Isaac received his name (which means *laughter*) from the fact that his mother had laughed when she was told she would bear a child at her advanced age. Amos, as we saw earlier, pleaded for his people by appealing to the name *Jacob*. At first it worked: " 'It shall not be,' said the Lord.'' But as Israel continued to sin, the covenant was turned into a joke. Therefore the Lord dropped the name *Jacob* and put the name *Isaac* in its place. The nation that turns its relationship with God into a joke will become the object of His holy laughter, as He destroys Isaac's high places.

Israel's religion had indeed become a joke. The Israelites liked to talk about their "fathers." Numerous pilgrims visited Beersheba (5:5), the holy place where the Lord had once revealed Himself to their forefather Isaac. Yet the spirit of their fathers was foreign to them.

Furthermore, not only their deformed church was to be destroyed, but also their *state*. The judgment did not apply just to their sanctuaries, but also to the house of Jeroboam. The king and the nation, the palace and the temple, the state and the church would be wiped out in the fire of judgment, just as at the last judgment.

It might seem that when the kingdom of the Antichrist comes, the "totalitarian" state will succeed in swallowing the church as it takes total control. But this is mere *appearance,* for when Christ returns, rulers will vacate their thrones and lay down their scepters as they kneel before the King whose Kingdom is not of this earth.

As I have said, both the state and the church will be torn down. Of course you realize that I mean the deformed church. The Church as the Body of Christ will never be destroyed. I do not mean to imply that its members are perfectly holy or that there is no disobedience reflected in the condition of its walls. On the contrary, those who are in the Church complain most of all about what has become of Zion.

This Church will be preserved only because it knows and believes that its King was measured with a plumb line, that He was torn down like a badly sagging wall, that He was battered and earned the name *Man of sorrows*. Although He was perfect, He was made to pay for what's wrong with our walls.

Through faith in Him and communion with Him, the crooked is made straight, and the sagging wall is repaired. The walls of Jerusalem are rebuilt. Anyone who takes the name of Jesus on his lips must forsake all unrighteousness. The plumb line of God's ordinances then becomes the rule that directs his life of gratitude.

30.
Shrines and
Sacred Cows

Never again prophesy at Bethel, for it is the king's sanctuary (7:13).

Amos finally got embroiled in an open conflict with the authorities. For a long time, people could smell something brewing. Amos's enemies scratched their heads and asked each other what could be done to make this prophet of doom shut up. As Amos went on and on, his preaching became intolerable. The smouldering opposition suddenly flared up as Amos's enemies took a radical step: they saw to it that he was forbidden to preach. No longer would he be allowed in the pulpit of the church at Bethel. In effect he was deported. The conflict took on a concrete form.

We almost feel like saying, "It's about time!" The deadly silence of the people must have bothered Amos as much as his prophetic warnings bothered them. It would have been unbearable for Amos if the stony silence had continued forever. Amos longed for some response, even if his preaching did infuriate them. He wanted their reaction, even if it meant that they would hurl abuse at him. He couldn't stand their silence.

At long last he heard their reaction. He didn't hear what he would like to have heard, namely, an expression of regret and a confession of guilt. But it was a reaction all the same, and who could say what the eventual outcome might be? An aroused Saul (Paul) imprisoning Christians is closer to the Kingdom of Heaven than an indifferent Laodicean who is neither hot nor cold.

It was Amaziah, the priest at Bethel, who spoke on behalf of the nation and verbalized the general attitude toward Amos's preaching: "Go away, seer; get back to the land of Judah; earn your bread there, do your prophesying there. We want no more prophesying in Bethel; this is the royal sanctuary, the national temple" (7:12-13 JB).

This, in any event, put an end to Amos's uncertainty about the effect of his preaching. He now knew what kind of impression he had made. The prophet was chased away. They told him he could preach as much as he liked in Judah, his own country, where there were doubtless a few things to be set straight, but from now on he was to remain silent in Bethel. He was not to mock Israel's "shrines," for Bethel was "the royal sanctuary, the national temple."

At first it seems strange that the series of visions in the book of Amos is interrupted by an account of the conflict between Amos and Amaziah. This story seems out of place between the vision of the plumb line (7:7-9) and that of the basket of summer fruit (8:1-3), to which the prophet turns after this interlude. The explanation for this is that Amos seems to have been literally interrupted by Amaziah as he was preaching. The crowd was definitely stirred by the sermon, and therefore Bethel's priest stopped Amos in the middle of his account of his prophetic visions.

How did this happen? Amos was not a preacher with a pulpit of his own. He proclaimed his message of judgment wherever the Lord sent him.

One day his voice was heard in the streets of Bethel. There is some ground for assuming that the occasion was the great harvest festival held on the fifteenth day of the month of Bul (I Kings 6:38). This was the national day of thanksgiving. Israel had again enjoyed a year of prosperity. That its wealth had been acquired through treachery and force was surely no reason not to praise the Lord for His generosity and offer sacrifices to Him. Bethel was *not* the place where the Lord chose to dwell, but this did not stop the crowd from crying out that it was indeed the temple of the Lord. Thus Bethel went ahead with its religious festival.

But now Amos appeared at this festival to spoil the celebration. He addressed the people and told them about the locusts and the fire and the plumb line and all the other frightening things the Lord had shown him. Amaziah was in the audience. His blood vessels almost burst with rage as he heard what Amos had to say about the altars at Bethel. When Amos added that it was his own intercession that had led the Lord to change His mind about the locust plague, Amaziah could hardly contain himself.

He was afraid Amos would soon become a second Elijah in the eyes of the people, because of his claim that he had influenced heaven through his prayers. Perhaps Amaziah would then suffer the fate of the priests of Baal, who were slaughtered by Elijah. At best Amaziah would be left alone in his beautiful temple with his sacred cow. His source of income would be gone. Amaziah himself was guilty of the charge he hurled at Amos when he accused him of prophesying to make a living! How he steamed inside! That man would have to be shut up somehow.

That farmer from Tekoa is getting even more insolent. First he talks about reducing the high places of Isaac to ruins and destroying the sanctuaries of Israel, and now he

says, "Sword in hand, I will attack the House of Jeroboam."
That's open revolution! He doesn't shrink from threatening
the *king* and his house. This violation of the king's sanctity
is high treason! That man is dangerous to the state!

Was it not the duty of Amaziah, as chief bishop, as the
priest honored by the king himself, to let Jeroboam know
about these revolutionary statements? The wily priest had
found just what he was looking for! There was no better
way for Amos to get himself into trouble than by using the
name of the *king* so boldly. Now it was only a minor detail
for Amaziah to mobilize the king's soldiers and use the
strong arm of the government to deport this pesky foreigner.
Amaziah should have been grateful to Amos for mentioning
Jeroboam in his sermon!

But Amaziah's devotion to the house of Jeroboam was
not as pure and innocent as one might suppose. His own
position as priest at Bethel was worth a great deal to him,
and Amos's preaching had jeopardized it. Yet Amaziah
could hardly voice this fear! It seemed much more prudent
to him to defend his own position by raising the royal flag
aloft and answering Amos's words with an appeal for loyalty
to the established church and the government. There have
been more Amaziahs in human history, masking their own
interests behind such noble appeals.

Hardly had Amos mentioned the name of the *king* when
Amaziah knew just what to do. He left the audience and
instructed a swift messenger to go to the king in Samaria and
report: "Amos is plotting against you in the heart of the
House of Israel; the country can no longer tolerate what he
keeps saying. For this is what he says, 'Jeroboam is going to
die by the sword, and Israel go into exile far from its country' "
(7:10-11 JB).

This is an old story that has been repeated again and
again. Wasn't Jeremiah also accused of treason? Wasn't
Christ called a revolutionary? Wasn't He accused of inciting
the people to rebellion and speaking out against Caesar?
Weren't the early Christians regarded as dangerous to the

state? Haven't church reformers often been branded revolutionaries disturbing the peace? Haven't the Christians of Nazi Germany and Communist Russia been accused of attacking everything sacred to the state? Those Christians must be silenced. The gospel must be blocked, for it hinders the building of our shrines, our sacred cows. If the force of reason won't do the trick, then we'll use the power of the state or the strong arm of the government — by simply forbidding Amos to preach at Bethel.

Meanwhile, Amaziah did not seem entirely certain that his plan would work. He could not be sure that Jeroboam would send his soldiers immediately. Jeroboam was a descendant of Nimshi (II Kings 9:14), and it was one of the traditions of that family not to oppose a prophet and his followers openly.

While awaiting Jeroboam's response, Amaziah still tried to get rid of Amos on his own, not by force but by persuasion. After sending his messenger to the king, he returned to where Amos was preaching and said, "Go away, seer; get back to the land of Judah." He meant: flee, before Jeroboam's soldiers arrest you. He tried to show Amos that it was in his interest to flee. There was no need for Amos to stop prophesying. That was his occupation, his way of earning a living, just as Amaziah earned his living by being a priest. The question of a livelihood was uppermost in Amaziah's mind and he considered it the strongest argument in his appeal to Amos.

This same rotten spirit manifested by Amaziah is still present in the church of Christ today. There are some people who think that preachers have a job just like anyone else. Actually, it's a job that pays too well. Rebellion and dissatisfaction can always be stirred up in the church by saying, "Those preachers have it made! It's a shame that so much of the money given to the church winds up in their pockets. But they are in the business for the money, after all." That sort of talk has the effect of robbing the Word of its power. There's nothing the devil enjoys more than the spectacle of church members arguing and complaining about the salaries paid to preachers. At such times the devil finds plenty of people like Amaziah to do his work for him.

Thus there was no need for Amos to stop prophesying. Everyone has to earn a living, and Amaziah had no intention of blocking Amos's pursuit of worldly gain. But he did insist that Amos do his prophesying in Judah, his own country, and not in Israel. Wouldn't it be wiser for Amos to limit his territory somewhat if he would be safer that way?

Amaziah appeared liberal and generous enough in his outlook. Amos was allowed to keep his own views, provided he would agree to propagate them elsewhere. Bethel, after all, was the king's sanctuary and the national place of worship. Amos should confine his prophesying to Judah. We sense in this argument something of the modern idea that religion is a private matter. There is a place for everything, but Bethel was not the place for Amos's kind of preaching.

Thus we can see what the real issue was. Amaziah wanted to protect his sacred cow at Bethel. He didn't want to give up the religious money tree he had carefully cultivated there. He was afraid Amos's preaching might cost him his position at Bethel. Therefore he said to Amos, "Keep your hands off my wife and stay out of my life. I can defend myself!"

Our own time abounds with shrines and sacred cows too. Traditional liberal politics is one of them. We are told, "You're welcome to your Bible, but don't bring it into public life. Stay home in Judah, and don't bother us at Bethel, for it's the king's sanctuary. Don't introduce doctrine into the schools, and don't poison the minds of our children. Don't bother us with any Christian ideas about social and political life, for that would degrade religion!"

Hitler's Third Reich was also full of shrines and sacred cows. The "state" was the "temple," the "king's sanctuary." If the prophets did not wish to join in the chorus of those who glorified the state, they would have to remain silent. In any event, they were not to protest. There was always some Amaziah or other to serve as priest on behalf of the state and see to it that dissenters were deported. The concentration camps were also available.

The "united" church, open to all, is a sacred cow as well. Amos would be welcome in such a church. This "Bethel," this "house of God," leaves its doors wide open to all. Its rooms are as spacious as the hearts of its people. If Amos cares to enter, he will be welcomed, but then he must learn to work with Amaziah in a fraternal way. He must keep his peculiar views and strict doctrines to himself, for they do not fit in with a man-made religion centered around a sacred cow.

Whenever we seek to uphold our own private "principles" at all costs, we, too, are worshipping a sacred cow. When we *refuse* to give up some sinful habit and *refuse* to bend to the discipline of God's Word, we are bowing down before a shrine.

Despite our promise to make our homes and lives a Bethel, a house of God, we eventually conclude that the house of God is really a fearful place and the voice of God a burden. We would much rather create some royal sanctuary where we ourselves will determine what to do and what not to do.

And when the preaching of God's Word makes it too hot for us, we think to ourselves, without quite daring to say it aloud: "Go away, seer! Tend to your own affairs and leave me alone." After the sermon, we leave the house of God (Bethel) and return to our day-to-day affairs, with the walls of our own little Bethel unshaken.

The prophet responds to this attitude by telling us what God thinks of it:

> You say, "Do not prophesy against Israel,
> and do not preach against the house of Isaac."
> Therefore thus says the Lord:
> "Your wife shall be a harlot in the city,

and your sons and daughters shall fall by the sword,
and your land shall be parceled out by line;
you yourself shall die in an unclean land,
and Israel shall surely go into exile away from its land'' (7:16-17).

The prophet's response to Amaziah was not limited to a personal defense. Amos did point out that he was not dependent on prophecy for his income, for he had enough income as a prosperous farmer. He also stated that he prophesied only at the Lord's command and on His authority, for the Lord *took* him from following the flocks (7:14-15). After this personal defense, Amos took the *offensive*. He told Amaziah that he and his house would be the hardest hit when the national catastrophe came. Furthermore, Israel would surely be driven out of its own land into exile.

It sounds like the same old thing again. We know that Cicero used to conclude his speeches in the Roman senate — in season and out of season — by declaring that Carthage must be destroyed. Amos was a holy counterpart of this heathen orator. He was a master of the holy art of preaching the Word — in season and out of season. Again and again he prophesied that Israel would be destroyed! Let's listen to him carefully!

31.
The Still Life

Thus the Lord God showed me: behold, a basket of summer fruit (8:1).

The beginning of Amos 8 certainly paints an idyllic picture for us: "Thus the Lord God showed me: behold, a basket of summer fruit. And he said, 'Amos, what do you see?' And I said, 'A basket of summer fruit.' "

Just after Amaziah interrupted Amos so rudely and abruptly, advising him to pack his bags and leave, Amos told the people at Bethel that he had seen a beautiful still life, a basket of ripe fruit. What was Amos up to? Was this wilderness prophet so shaken by the words of warning that he changed his tune to suit Amaziah? Was he substituting a vision of a glorious future for his prophecy of doom?

Surely a basket of fruit couldn't mean doom. Fruit is

nothing to be afraid of! First there was the spring vision of the locusts devouring the young, green crops, signifying a frightful famine. Then there was the summer vision of the great fire consuming everything — another catastrophe. Then came the vision of the plumb line, in which Israel was compared to a sagging wall that would have to be torn down as quickly as possible.

But now the prophet was apparently singing a different song. Because of the threats of the priest and his fear of the king's soldiers, he quickly painted a beautiful picture of Israel, an autumn scene. He depicted Israel as a beautiful basket of ripe fruit. Everyone loves the sight of a basket of fruit. That's what you look like, Israel — a basket of fruit!

This might *appear* to be what Amos meant, but he actually had something quite different in mind. We already know Amos too well to even suspect him of *retreating* so quickly.

It's likely that Amos himself didn't grasp the meaning of this autumn vision right away. This vision needed divine explanation even more than the vision of the plumb line. In the latter vision Amos could tell immediately that something was amiss, for one does not measure and check a wall that stands erect on its foundations. But who would think of something frightening when he sees a basket of ripe fruit?

The Lord explained what the vision meant. It's as simple as saying hello. "My people Israel is ripe for destruction; I will no longer overlook its offenses" (8:2 JB). The similarity between the summer fruit and the people of Israel is that both were *ripe*. The fruit in the basket was *ripe* and ready to eat, while Israel was *ripe* for judgment. It was too late to escape.

Amos went on to explain how horrible the judgment would be: " 'The songs in the temple shall become wailings in that day,' says the Lord God. 'The dead bodies shall be many; in every place they shall be cast out in silence' " (8:3).

It's a sobering catastrophe — just like the house in

which ten people died. But the resulting silence is not that of the uncle who asks for silence because of his idolatrous fear of mentioning the name of Yahweh. The prophet calls for a respectful silence in the presence of all those dead bodies. We should not speak when God stretches out His hand in judgment.

This still life (the basket of fruit) depicting Israel hits the nail on the head in more than one way. Israel seemed in excellent condition — on the surface. Everything appeared to be going well. Numerous offerings were brought. The religious ceremonies were observed scrupulously, and the sabbath was carefully kept. The life of Israel seemed to be full of beauty and piety. Surely God must love this chosen nation. Israel was just like a painting! Just as one would love to take a bite of the ripe fruit, one would like to embrace those pious Israelites and kiss them. That's how earnest their godliness seemed. It's enough to make you green with envy!

That's how it looked from the outside. But the inner condition of the people made them ripe for judgment, just as the fruit was ripe for eating. Amos describes their condition by pointing to what was going on in their minds. They were thinking:

> When will the new moon be over,
> that we may sell grain?
> And the sabbath,
> that we may offer wheat for sale? (8:5).

They were most scrupulous and punctual about keeping the sabbath — no question about it! Never would they violate the sabbath by buying and selling. Wasn't someone once stoned for gathering wood on the sabbath?

The wealthy grain buyers joined very piously in the prayers and songs of the temple. They sang of their yearning to enter God's house, and they sang that their souls were consumed by a desire to praise the Lord.

That's what they sang. But if you could also read their

minds, you would realize that what they really desired was
not God but gold. They thought to themselves, "When will
this endless sabbath be over? How slowly the sabbath day
passes!" Those grain dealers did indeed close their places of
business, but they were most reluctant to do so. The service
of God didn't interest them in the slightest, for the service
of gold occupied all their attention.

Yet there is still something that could be said in their
defense. Life with its pressing demands is busy and absorbing.
Sometimes it's extremely difficult to forget all about business
as the collection plate is being passed in church. It is understandable that the rustle of dollar bills and the tinkle of coins
sometimes draws our attention momentarily. Let someone
who never sins on this count cast the first stone at the grain
dealers.

But — that's not all that went on in the minds of
these businessmen. The prophet tells us that they were not
thinking only about opening the doors of their businesses
again. They were also eager for the moment when they could
actually sell their grain, for then they could "make the ephah
small and the shekel great, and deal deceitfully with false
balances" (8:5). Thus, in the temple they were filled with
amusement at the prospect of deceiving people. They would
trick them both ways; they would get them coming and going.

The shekel was used to weigh the coins which the customers used to pay for their purchases. When these grain
dealers weighed their customers' coins, they would use an
extra-large shekel as a counterweight. Then they could shake
their heads and declare that the coins offered were not of
the proper weight. The customer would have to pay a little
more! On the one hand, then, the buyers would get less grain
than they were promised — the grain dealers would use a
small ephah to measure the grain — and on the other hand,
they would pay too much for it.

Thus the grain dealers had reason to smirk and wink at
each other in the temple. Their bag of tricks also included
using scales deceitfully. The very thought of these tricks

sometimes made them laugh out loud in the temple. Then they would put on a serious face again and listen to the law and the prophets being read. What was it that Amaziah was saying? False weights and measures are an abomination in the sight of the Lord! Amen!

The sabbath thoughts of these grain dealers went even further. Impatiently they waited for the sabbath to end, so that they could "buy the poor for silver and the needy for a pair of sandals, and sell the refuse of the wheat" (8:6). They would reach their goal when they had not only taken the poor man's last penny but robbed him of his freedom as well. Those grain dealers went so far that the poor finally had to sell themselves into slavery to the wealthy swindlers.

The contrast is most striking when Amos tells us what they were thinking: "We *buy people* for money, and *sell refuse* as grain." They saw to it that what they bought was sound, but what they sold wasn't. It wasn't even grain: it was garbage.

Some older translations suggest that the refuse spoken of here is chaff. Going this far, however, would certainly have hurt the business of these swindlers. Therefore we should think instead of grain of a very poor quality. They sold the poorest grain as the best. Here we see again that the sinful practice of lying about a product to be sold is as old as the selfish heart of man.

This still life that looked so beautiful at first glance was not all that it appeared to be, then. The nation was indeed ripe for judgment.

Appearances in our own lives and society can be equally deceptive. To someone examining us outwardly, we all seem so pious. The life of the church is as beautiful as a painting. The church is full each Sunday morning. Evangelism and missionary work are supported enthusiastically. There are youth organizations and hymnsings. The doctrines of the church are defended zealously. Truly we are watchmen on Zion's walls.

But it's more important to inquire into what we think than what we say. What lives in our hearts is more important than the motions we go through or the sabbath day we observe. God knows what's in our hearts, just as Amos knew and announced what those grain dealers were thinking.

Now, no one would argue that what we do — as opposed to what we think — is of no importance. Yet we should ask whether those grain dealers might not feel at home in today's Jerusalem and Samaria, and whether the deviousness in which they excelled is perhaps present in our lives.

Let's not say too much about it. It's enough to say to God: "Look into my heart and soul, Lord, to see if there is anything evil hidden there, and set my feet on the path leading to blessedness and righteousness." Let us test ourselves, so that when the command is given to the angels to gather in the world's harvest, we will not be ripe for judgment, but will be brought into the eternal barns. This is the message behind the basket of ripe fruit, the admonition in Amos's vision of the still life.

Let's hope that for us the still life will become an uneasy and troubled life. That was also what Amos had in mind: he wanted to shake those who were living the still and peaceful life on the mountain of Samaria out of their complacency. Becoming troubled is the first step toward true peace, the peace of the sabbath, the peace that will never be interrupted by the question: "When will this sabbath ever end?"

32.
Cut the Knot

I saw the Lord standing at the side of the altar. "Strike the capitals," he said, "and let the roof tumble down!" (9:1 JB).

We now turn our attention to the fifth and last of Amos's visions, which represents a striking prefiguration of the last judgment. The line of thought it contains leads to the Apostles' Creed and the idea that Christ will return "to judge the living and the dead."

What Amos saw was simply the Lord standing by the altar. But the prophet didn't just *see* the Lord; he also *heard* Him give a command to someone unnamed and unseen. (The name of God used here is not the covenant name but *Adonai,* which means *the one who governs everything.*) The anonymous agent of God's will was probably one of the devasta-

ting natural forces under "Adonai's" command. He is presented as a person and receives the following command:

> Strike the capitals, and let the roof tumble down!
> I mean to break their heads, every one,
> and all who remain I will put to the sword;
> not one shall get away,
> not one escape.

Amos sees the temple full of people. It is the sabbath
day, or perhaps a festival day. Presumably the grain dealers
for whom the sabbath goes by so slowly are in the audience.
There are also many priests. There is much singing and sacrificing. I leave to the professional exegetes the question
whether we are to think here of the temple in Jerusalem or
the temple in Samaria. In any event, things were not much
better in Jerusalem than in Samaria, with its man-made
religion.

Suddenly the Lord appears at the altar. Something
must be wrong! If the scene is Jerusalem, where the Lord
still wished to dwell in His temple, there is reason for concern,
for His dwelling place is the Holy of Holies. For Him to
appear *elsewhere* in the temple would mean that He has left
His place of rest. Does He plan to leave the temple entirely?
Is He dissatisfied with the sacrifices at the "altar"? In any
event, He appears as the Almighty at the altar. Thus there is
reason to tremble. And if the scene is Samaria, the temple
where religion was tailored to suit man, there is even more
to worry about. The very appearance of the Lord would
already seal the fate of the temple.

Various aspects of this vision make me think of a royal
wedding feast, and especially of the moment when the king
himself appears. It is a dramatic moment, a time for hypocrites to be silent. And the temple, of course, was full of
hypocrisy; it was full of people who observed the sabbath
day scrupulously and brought abundant offerings, thinking
all the while, "When will this sabbath ever end?"

From whichever angle we look at this scene, the picture
is grim. "I saw the Lord standing at the side of the altar."

Listen! The Lord is saying something! Hardly has He spoken than His command is executed. He issues an order, and a mighty cyclone arises to "cut the knot," so that the whole building shakes. This knot must have been part of a cord holding all the crossbeams together. Once it is cut, the pillars can no longer support the roof resting upon them. The people in the temple die a horrible death as the roof and the walls collapse. What a frightful scene!

The temple was a place of *blessing,* and the altar with its horns gave asylum to fugitives. But if one enters the temple — or the church — with the wrong purposes in mind, the blessing becomes a *curse.* The Word and the sacraments then have a destructive effect. Such a person is killed by his own sins and buried in the temple.

Not everyone at the temple feast dies immediately. "All who remain I will put to the sword," we read. This is a reference to those who didn't get a place in the front pews but stood in the back or perhaps outside the temple. The Israelites were "pious" and attended the services in the temple in great numbers. So many showed up that there wasn't room for all of them inside the temple. "Church life is booming," declared those who watched attendance figures but forgot to test the spirits.

Those who sit at the front are killed first. Those who sit in the back and survive the collapse of the building flee in vain. With horrible realism, Amos describes how the wrath of the Lord tracks these fugitives down. (I will come back to this a little later.)

It might be asked why the Lord did this in the temple of His covenant people instead of in the heathen temples, where such awful things went on. Surely there were even more things in need of correction — or destruction — among the heathens. Their wickedness cried out to heaven.

God did indeed see and hear all of that heathen wickedness. But let's not concern ourselves at this point with God's wrath directed toward the "world." All of that will come. God forgets nothing and overlooks nothing. But we can be sure that He won't overlook the sins of His people either. The judgment will begin with Jerusalem.

To settle the matter, Amos quotes God as follows: "My eyes will be on them for their misfortune, not their good" (9:4 JB). We must remember that God always pays special attention to His people. He blesses them more readily than He blesses the world, but He also punishes them more severely. "It shall be more tolerable for Tyre and Sidon on the day of judgment than for you" (Matt. 11:22).

God's frightening wrath was directed especially against "the altar." That was why He stood beside it. The altar was the central offense, so to speak; it was the final, compelling proof of Israel's guilt.

The altar is always the midpoint and heart of a religion. No religion is conceivable without an altar. The altar is central especially in Christianity, with its emphasis on sacrifice. Think of the sacrifice made by Christ, and the thanksgiving offerings made by believers. Therefore it's all the more distressing when that midpoint or heart is corrupted. Any religion in which this happens is suffering from a serious illness. A religion without an altar is no real religion, and a religion with a desecrated altar is a caricature of religion.

Israel's altar had been desecrated. Yet it had not been taken away. On the contrary, the country was full of altars built contrary to God's express desires. This very profusion of altars represented a sin against "the altar." The religion which the Israelites had devised for themselves was an attempt to kill the true religion.

David had said that the sacrifice pleasing to God is a broken heart and a contrite spirit, but later Israelites had forgotten that, just as they had forgotten Samuel's statement that obeying the voice of the Lord is better than sacrificing the fat of rams. What they laid on the altar was not a thankful and devoted heart but the flesh of cattle and goats. They thought the Lord took great pleasure in such sacrifices.

Thus the altar, the central token of godliness in the temple, became a finger pointed at Israel in accusation. It is against this background that we must consider the command to cut the knot and let the roof tumble down.

Therefore this Word spoken by Amos should also cause us to tremble. What would happen today if the Lord came down in all His holiness to look at our altars and what we lay on them? We as churchgoers are so busy building altars and making sacrifices and raising the banner of the cross in "all areas of life"! But God is opposed to altars in temples where religion is mere appearance, where the heart is missing, where upright devotion is absent. He will show us how *dangerous* it is to stand right by the altar. The priests were the first ones to lose their lives in the catastrophe.

It is better to stay away from altars and the smell of incense entirely than to come to the Lord's temple with a heart that is not contrite, bringing sacrifices and declaring that they are for the Lord. Let's think about it seriously. Although our private altars may still be standing, there will come a day of reckoning, which the prophet Amos describes in rich Old Testament imagery:

> Should they burrow their way down to Sheol,
> my hand shall haul them out;
> should they scale the heavens,
> I will drag them down;
> should they hide on Carmel's peak,
> there I will track them down and catch them;
> should they hide from my sight on the sea bed,
> I will tell the Dragon to bite them there;
> should they go into exile driven before their enemies,
> I will order the sword to slaughter them there (9:2-4 JB).

All that we have been and done will be revealed before the judgment seat of Christ. The prophet informs us that there will not be a single place in the whole creation where we can hide from the Judge of the entire earth.

To make this clear, Amos cites a few examples. It may be that during such a catastrophe as the earthquake, some Israelites would seek refuge on the top of Mount Carmel, hoping to escape the wrath by hiding in the thick bushes and

deep caves. But even there the Lord's hand would find them.
It may be that some Israelites would prefer death in the water
to falling into the hands of the Lord. Thus they might flee
from the top of Carmel into the Mediterranean Sea. Yet
Yahweh would order a huge sea monster to track them down
at the bottom of the sea. Even the hiding places impossible
to reach could not conceal anyone from the Judge of heaven
and earth:

> Though they dig into Sheol,
> from there my hand shall take them up;
> though they climb up to heaven,
> from there I will bring them down (9:2).

God sees them all!

Since the days of Amos, such places beyond man's
reach have been brought a bit closer through technological
achievements. Man digs deep passageways into the earth and
seeks protection in underground bunkers and bomb shelters
— protection from his *fellow man*! But these bunkers will
not protect him from God. With airplanes and rockets he
has learned how to travel to the outer reaches of the earth's
atmosphere and beyond it, but he does not know how to
enter heaven. Technology and culture have not brought
about heaven on earth, either. The cultured man of the
twentieth century is proud of such achievements as precision
bombing from airplanes high in the sky and the long-range
missiles that sow destruction in an incredibly effective way,
but he does not know how to escape God's punishment.

The man who has never learned to pray but has always
put his faith in human culture will ultimately pray in terror
for the hills and mountains, which cannot hear and will not
be moved, to fall upon him. Then all we have been and
done will be revealed before the judgment seat of Christ!

In this great universe, there is but one safe place —
Golgotha! There the command to cut the knot was given
long ago. The mountains shook and the rocks were rent.

There the Lord was crushed on the altar. There all of God's wrath was burnt out. Golgotha is both a horrible and blessed place!

He who seeks to save his life need not look for a hiding place in the heights or the depths, nor need he travel the length and breadth of the land. Let him flee instead to the hill of the cross, where God shook the earth to its foundations, where the waters were turbulent because of the church's sin against the altar. Yet that place of turbulence is also a place of peace for all sinners and murderers. "Today you shall be with Me in Paradise."

33.
The Fallen House
and the Palace

*On that day I will restore David's fallen house
(9:11 NEB).*

The preaching of the farmer from Tekoa is made up of
one threat after another. On all sides we see the storm clouds
forming. We hear the dull rumble of the thunder of judgment. From the trumpet issues a far from uncertain sound
announcing some frightening news: the enemy is on the way!

But when Amos finishes his lengthy appeal for repentance, he cannot resist the impulse to lay aside the trumpet
for a moment and play the flute. The sun breaks through the
clouds briefly. Its light shines on Canaan's pastures in better
days, days

> when harvest will follow directly after plowing,
> the treading of grapes soon after sowing,

when the mountains will run with new wine
and the hills all flow with it (9:13 JB).

My cup runneth over!

> I mean to restore the fortunes of my people Israel;
> they will rebuild the ruined cities and live in them,
> plant vineyards and drink their wine,
> dig gardens and eat their produce.
> I will plant them in their own country,
> never to be rooted up again
> out of the land I have given them,
> says Yahweh, your God (9:14-15 JB).

God does have mercy on His people!

Thus Amos holds the key to the Kingdom of Heaven
not just to slam the door in the face of unbelievers but also
to open it for believers, by announcing and testifying to all
of them openly that their sins have been forgiven for Christ's
sake.

This announcement must have been a great relief and
joy to Amos, who had such a burden to bear, who had to
proclaim judgment on God's behalf. We have seen him
weeping as he called down God's fire on the palaces of
Samaria and Jerusalem. He wept in sorrow over what had
become of *his* people. But now we see him weeping with joy
when God allows him to say:

> On that day I will restore
> David's fallen house;
> I will repair its gaping walls and restore its ruins;
> I will rebuild it as it was long ago.

The judgment and the promise do not contradict one
another. Amos was preaching both destruction and the
good news of restoration. The kingdom of heaven will be
opened to believers and closed to unbelievers. Those who are
at ease in Zion will be destroyed, while those who are
troubled will rejoice.

What Amos said about the restoration of David's house was certainly a reason for the troubled of Zion to rejoice. But it was also an occasion for feeling chastened. After all, Amos spoke of David's house as *fallen*. It was a house full of holes and cracks; it looked like the dilapidated dwelling of a pauper.

Yet that's hardly what it looked like during the time of Amos. On the contrary, David's kingdom was more prosperous than ever before. But Amos was a prophet; he could see the insides of things and could look into the future. When he looked *within,* he saw that everything behind the beautiful facade was decayed and rotten. Had the Lord not shown him with a plumb line that the wall was sagging?

When Amos looked into the future, he saw a time when David's descendants would be deported to the last man and nothing would be left of the great oak but a stump. The king and queen of the house of David would no longer be dressed in splendid, purple garments. The king would be a carpenter, and the queen would be surrounded by animals as she gave birth to her child. This fallen house of David presents a picture of extreme poverty!

It is certainly tragic that Amos, who lived some 250 years after the glorious reign of David and Solomon, had to speak of this once splendid *palace* as a *fallen house.* We can hardly think of a greater contrast or a deeper fall.

Perhaps we could speak here of "the ravages of time." Is there anything abiding here on earth? Doesn't every palace eventually become a run-down ruin? What is left of such ancient world-cities as Babel and Nineveh? What do we find in Rome and Athens? Ruins! Who recognizes the handsome young man of fifty years ago in the doddering old man moving slowly down the street? Haven't crown princes gone into exile? What has become of the rulers of the old German and Russian empires? Haven't famous business corporations gone bankrupt? Aren't there farmers who were once masters on their own land that are now reduced to selling worthless merchandise from door to door? Who is strong enough to resist the currents of change?

David's fallen house is the home of a family of paupers. Is there something wrong with that? Are we so much better than the people who live in such fallen houses? Is someone who spends the last years of his life in a comfortable home in the country so much better than someone else who breathes his last breath on a straw mattress? Must we accept the impoverished logic of popular opinion when it declares that someone who is *better off* than someone else is also *better?*

No, we should not scorn Israel for its poverty. Yet we shouldn't forget that poverty did bring shame on David's house. A palace can collapse and become a ruin. A business can go downhill without the owner being able to do anything about it. "It's no crime to be poor," we then say.

But it can also happen that someone wilfully neglects his opportunities and wastes his goods and property. In such a case, there is indeed something wrong with being poor!

Israel's poverty falls into the latter category. The fallen house is an open reproach to its owner, for it is the result of his neglect and wastefulness. It didn't have to happen. Hadn't the Lord promised David that He would establish his descendants forever? Yet with this promise came a warning:

> If his children forsake my law
> and do not walk according to my ordinances,
> if they violate my statutes
> and do not keep my commandments,
> then I will punish their transgression with the rod
> and their iniquity with scourges (Ps. 89:30-2).

This warning had been disregarded, and therefore punishment was due. The Israelites lived in luxury, drinking wine by the bowlful and lying on couches in houses of ivory. God's generous gifts were being squandered. The Israelites seemed to think there was no end to them. They sought prosperity, but they did not look to God as the Giver of all good gifts. This way of life could not last and would soon lead to ruin and condemnation.

Thus it would not be correct to say that God brought about the ruin of the palace. Nor can the blame for Israel's destruction be laid at the doorstep of its enemies Edom and Tyre, even though this might seem a likely explanation. (Doesn't the world always seek to destroy the church?) This was not the problem in Israel's case; in fact, God was so long-suffering in the time of Amos that He still gave Israel victories over its enemies.

No, what had seemed impossible and incomprehensible had actually happened: the inhabitants of the palace were the ones who ruined it. Because of their wastefulness and injustice, holes began to appear in the walls. They didn't bother to keep the palace clean and in good order. Finally God simply put His *seal* upon their neglect by burying the inhabitants of the palace under the ruins they had created. He made them live in a fallen house instead. That was what these descendants of kings had been begging for, in effect.

In Amos's words about the church of the old covenant, there is a frightening accusation that applies to the New Testament church as well. There is a serious danger that the *poverty of the church* may somehow be regarded as proper and may even be idealized. That the church has so little influence in this world, that its lack of faith and unity robs it of the importance it should have, that it goes its own way like a small band of inconspicuous people, all of this is attributed to the devil and the enemies of the church. Therefore it's time we opened our eyes to the sinful poverty we have *chosen*! The walls are in need of repair not so much because of the church's enemies as because of its own members. The quarreling and jealousy inside the church cause breaches in its walls, as do the wish to be like the world and the desire to design our own religion.

That the churches no longer open and close heaven's doors, that they no longer crush the serpent, that they no longer cast out evil spirits is no one's fault but their own. It is the result of their neglect of prayer and their lack of faith. That the King's children go through life like forlorn beggars who sleep in hovels *may* be the fault of the church's enemies — as it is when Christians are forced to surrender their lives, when the believers in Smyrna are made to go hungry, and when no one is able to buy or sell in the time of the Antichrist unless he bears the mark of the Beast. More often, however, the cause can be found in the church members themselves.

As for the attack which the Antichrist will make on the church, he will not need all his strength. He will be attacking not a secure fortress but a church already decaying internally. The victory will be an easy one, just as Christ will win an easy victory over the Antichrist in the "fullness of time." Just as Hitler's Third Reich could only arise out of the ruins of a kingdom badly weakened by the spirit of revolution, so the kingdom of the Antichrist, which will be established from sea to sea, will come at a time when the church has the form of godliness but not its power, when the "army of Jesus Christ" is ready to put on the uniform of the Antichrist's army.

Then the Antichrist will rejoice, but his glee will be premature. He will assume that the church will no longer fight him because it has become a "fallen house," but he will be mistaken.

The gates of hell will not prevail against that fallen house. The church may sink very low. Many of its members will fall away, forcing Jesus to ask, "Will there be faith on earth?" But the church will never *disappear*. God will intervene in a *miraculous* way and prevent it.

He already did so when Christ came forth out of the stump of Jesse. Then the church of the New Testament rose from the fallen house of the old covenant. The fallen house was restored, and the gospel of Christ conquered the world.

This miracle will happen again "on that day." It may seem impossible for the fallen house of the church to hold out against the furious attack of the Antichrist. Yet this wonder will indeed take place. At the very moment when the beast of prey is about to seize the turtle dove, Christ with His many thousands of angels will chase away the Antichrist and his devils. The hosts of the evil one will be scattered and punished.

"On that day I will restore David's fallen house." I can see them building, just as they did long ago. But the restored palace will be even more beautiful.

Once the militant church has finally become the triumphant church and the fallen house has become a palace built on firm foundations — the Father's house with room for all, of which Jesus spoke — then there will be no earthly power capable of tearing down that palace. The inhabitants of the palace will not cause its ruin either, for they will be holy.

Have our lives been destroyed through our own sin? Have we become a fallen house? If so, we should remember that Amos, the prophet of doom, holds out hope for us, a hope that is well founded. God has promised to restore the fallen house of *David*. This indicates that He is a *covenant* God who has given a promise to David and all his children.

After hearing the voice of Amos reproach them as Nathan once reproached David, the children of David weep because of their sins. They pray to God and confess the magnitude of their guilt. They confess that the thought of their guilt never leaves them, and that they have deeply offended God with their numerous transgressions.

Amos also points to the answer: Jesus Christ. *He* was willing to take our poverty and shame upon Himself. *He* dwelt in the fallen house of our flesh because we ruined His palace.

"On that day I will restore David's fallen house!"

PUBLISHER'S NOTE

In the original Dutch edition of this book, Rev. Veldkamp acknowledges his dependence on the exegetical insights of Prof. C. van Gelderen, who has dealt with the book of Amos in *Het boek Amos,* published by J. H. Kok N. V. of Kampen.

Quotations from the Bible are taken from the Revised Standard Version unless otherwise indicated. Translations of the Heidelberg Catechism are taken from the new translation prepared by a committee of the Christian Reformed Church and published by its Board of Publications in 1975.